Advanced Introduction to Law and Literature

Elgar Advanced Introductions are stimulating and thoughtful introductions to major fields in the social sciences, business and law, expertly written by the world's leading scholars. Designed to be accessible yet rigorous, they offer concise and lucid surveys of the substantive and policy issues associated with discrete subject areas.

The aims of the series are two-fold: to pinpoint essential principles of a particular field, and to offer insights that stimulate critical thinking. By distilling the vast and often technical corpus of information on the subject into a concise and meaningful form, the books serve as accessible introductions for undergraduate and graduate students coming to the subject for the first time. Importantly, they also develop well-informed, nuanced critiques of the field that will challenge and extend the understanding of advanced students, scholars and policy-makers.

For a full list of titles in the series please see the back of the book. Recent titles in the series include:

National Accounting
John M. Hartwick

Legal Research Methods
Ernst Hirsch Ballin

Privacy Law
Megan Richardson

International Human Rights Law
Second Edition
Dinah L. Shelton

Law and Artificial Intelligence
Woodrow Barfield and Ugo Pagallo

Politics of International Human Rights
David P. Forsythe

Community-based Conservation
Fikret Berkes

Global Production Networks
Neil M. Coe

Mental Health Law
Michael L. Perlin

Law and Literature
Peter Goodrich

Advanced Introduction to

Law and Literature

PETER GOODRICH

Professor of Law and Director of the Program in Law and Humanities, Cardozo School of Law, New York, USA and Visiting Professor, School of Social Science, New York University Abu Dhabi, United Arab Emirates

Elgar Advanced Introductions

Edward Elgar
PUBLISHING

Cheltenham, UK • Northampton, MA, USA

© Peter Goodrich 2021

All rights reserved. No part of this publication may be reproduced, stored in a retrieval system or transmitted in any form or by any means, electronic, mechanical or photocopying, recording, or otherwise without the prior permission of the publisher.

Published by
Edward Elgar Publishing Limited
The Lypiatts
15 Lansdown Road
Cheltenham
Glos GL50 2JA
UK

Edward Elgar Publishing, Inc.
William Pratt House
9 Dewey Court
Northampton
Massachusetts 01060
USA

A catalogue record for this book
is available from the British Library

Library of Congress Control Number: 2020950866

This book is available electronically on *Elgar Advanced Introductions: Law*
www.advancedintros.com

ISBN 978 1 78990 599 1 (cased)
ISBN 978 1 78990 601 1 (paperback)
ISBN 978 1 78990 600 4 (eBook)

Typeset by Servis Filmsetting Ltd, Stockport, Cheshire
Printed and bound in Great Britain by TJ Books Limited, Padstow, Cornwall

Contents

List of figures	vi
Acknowledgements	vii
Prologue	viii
1 The republic of lawyers	1
2 The discipline of law	24
3 Allegories	42
4 Legal imaginations	67
5 Transitions	90
Epilogue	109
Index	115

Figures

4.1	*R v Frederick Henry Seddon*	74
4.2	His Honour Justice Picton	76
4.3	*Clare and Ors v Bedelis*	79
4.4	*Sikhs for Justice v Badal*	86
4.5	*Sikhs for Justice v Badal*	87

Acknowledgements

A pleiad of the most probative and approbative protreptic postulations to Marco Wan and to Sabarish Suresh who kindly read the manuscript in its entirety. My borrowings, acquisitions, entanglements, stylistic and other inspirations from the neoteric theoretical funambulism of Daniela Gandorfer are numerous. The work of Anne Teissier-Ensminger on jurisliterature has been pivotal to the argument of this book and so too, as ever, the historical excursions of Valérie Hayaert. The vehicular intuitions and jurisographic observations of Shaun McVeigh, and Desmond Manderson's aesthetic acumen were also important signposts. Marett Leiboff's intimate intellective and interpretative calisthenics opened new spaces. Much of the expansion of vocabulary was provided in conversations with Ronnie Goodrich. Inspirations from Linda Mills continue to exceed the scope of my confinement and the rigidity of my Englishness.

Prologue

An advanced introduction is one which advances the discipline and introduces novelty into the extant tradition and writings. 'Law and Literature', one of law's many copulative enterprises, is an expression that denotes a generous humanistic investment in apprehending and expanding the role of the jurist in the community of disciplines. The last half century, or close enough – James Boyd White's pioneering work *The Legal Imagination* was published in 1973 – has seen a renaissance of work, and a scholarly journal, devoted specifically, or at least nominally, to law and literature. There are Handbooks, Research Guides, Introductions, Critical Introductions, in this instance an Advanced Introduction, as well as innovative and less endurable volumes with titles such as *Poethics, Literary Criticisms of Law, New Directions in Law and Literature, From Law and Literature to Legality and Affect*, and even the finely paradoxical title *Lex Populi*, as guides to the confluence of disciplines.[1] It has also on occasion been pronounced dead on arrival by the literary scholar Julie Stone Peters whose diagnosis of demise, if correct, would appear to stall the advance before it has started.[2] What passes under the title 'law and literature', however, is simply one version and reprise, played well, done badly, as the case entails, of poetic jurisprudence and its rhetorical investigation and performance of the theatre of legality.

---

1 William P. MacNeil, Lex Populi: *The Jurisprudence of Popular Culture* (Palo Alto: Stanford University Press, 2007) is the most innovative and expansive of the texts, developing a notion of 'peoples's law' or 'pop law'. The supposition is languidly captured at 9: "Moving recklessly as I did across jurisdictions – from Oz to Blighty to the Land of E Pluribus Unum – this text shifts and swerves, back and forth, from the page to the screen; or in Lacanese, from the Symbolic (of words, of texts) to the Imaginary (of reflections, of mirror images). This kind of reckless abandon, however, is defensible because it is precisely this sort of peripatetic movement *lex populi* not only solicits but enacts, its principal effect being the very erasure of the distance between the word and the image."

2 Julie Stone Peters, 'Law, Literature, and the Vanishing Real: On the Future of an Interdisciplinary Illusion,' (2005) 120 *PMLA* 442. For elaboration of my views on this dialogue of disciplines, see Goodrich, 'Screening Law' (2009) 21(1) *Law and Literature* 1. On holes and the lure of other disciplines as cures for law's lack, see Maria Aristodemou, *Law, Psychoanalysis, Society: Taking the Unconscious Seriously* (Abingdon: Routledge, 2015).

The eponymous Professor Peters – she shares my very Christian name – is not entirely wrong. The 'and' of the subdiscipline can denote a desire for an imaginary other, a panacea or cure in the tenebrous interstices of an alien and alluring scholarly exoticism. In this depiction, Julie Stone's scythe in hand, literature will reinstate the research credentials and interpretative skills that lawyers have lost. Law will give the frivolous practitioners of literary criticism a gravitas of subject matter that they severely lack in the wake of the culture wars and the increasingly market driven orientation of the university. Neither dream came true. The marriage didn't last. Law for its part was busy having affairs with other disciplines, with economics, history, social science, and now trans studies, and theoretical physics. Literary criticism opted for post-criticism and settled down to enjoyment of the text, which rather precludes law. All of which simply indicates that focus on the copulative 'and' is a distraction. Introducing an advance means moving beyond the institutional squabbles and sub-disciplinary turf wars that serve to entertain the tenured but lack a properly humanistic scope of perspective upon the *longue durée* of jurisliterature.

Over the course of the last decades the French legal historian Anne Teissier-Ensminger has worked exhaustively in the elaboration of the concept of jurisliterature, which will be utilized extensively though divergently in the present book.[3] It is the affective and performative practices and possibilities of jurisliterature that will be engaged in the present study. Conceived more inventively as an imaginative and transitionally orientated embodiment of law's material practices, its atmospheric and spatial occupations, its fictions and mutations, the concept of the jurisliterary allow for the development of a more expansive and legally relevant concept of the literature of law as an aesthetic genre in its own right. Distinct from a *belle lettrist* concept of literary accounts of law which primarily addresses what canonic novelists, theatre and film, have had to say or portray of lawyers, jurisliterature looks to the long term of legal humanism and its didactic works, its systematizations, its enchiridions, preparatives, commentaries, the plurality of its discourses as a genre worthy of study in its own right.[4] This is not a

---

3 Anne Teissier-Ensminger, *La beauté du Droit* (Paris: Garnier, 1999); Teissier-Ensminger, *Le Droit incarné, huit parcours en jurislittérature* (Paris: Garnier, 2013); Teissier-Ensminger, *Fabuleuse juridicité. Sur la littérarisation des genres juridiques* (Paris: Garnier, 2015) are three principal works.
4 For anglophone work that takes up a comparable notion of law as a literary genre and culture, see Guyora Binder and Robert Weisberg, *Literary Criticisms of Law* (Princeton: Princeton University Press, 2018); Greig Henderson, *Creating Legal Worlds: Story and Style in a Culture of Argument*

question of the countless lawyers who have written fiction, theatrical works, film scripts, though these have their relevance, but rather a matter of the imaginative works of jurists, the pedagogic, institutional, substantive doctrinal and judicial writings that make up the corpus of a tradition of teaching and transmitting law, a *mos litteratus iuris docendi*. The exposition of law is always a literary, which is to say an imaginative endeavour, a rhetorical exercise, and jurisliterature is the term that best approximates to answering the crucial questions of legal humanism. At root the project is that of apprehending the extent to which the literature of law can satisfy aesthetic criteria, its affective and imaginal desiderata, its dramatic roles and performances, and still mingle amongst the erudite disciplines without abandoning the identities of the jurist to other and often more attractive pursuits. In the concept of jurisliterature and the expansiveness of its tradition of eloquence and elegance, erudition and invention, the wilder history of the juridical, of its poetical sermons, its amorous texts, its didactic fictions, lawyers are forced to recognize the role of the liberal arts, including literary and critical theory, performance and media studies, to the manner of understanding and the forms and figures of exposition of law's textual and other plastic and virtual elaborations.

Jurisliterature belongs to its time and place, to the mobile and mutating *corpus iuris* of a jurisdiction, to a complexity of traditions and institutions that promulgate, expatiate and interpret the juridical identities, practices and decisions of the legal system over time. Precedent, as the critics of common law are fond of announcing, is poor history but the jurisliterary point is that it is not history. Jurishistory is a literary invention and legal inscription of a geopolitical perspective, a certain nomos of the earth and its inhabitants.[5] It takes different forms over time and has distinctive cultural and national traditions. The Spanish tradition (*mos hispanicus iuris docendi*) mixes fiction with historical narrative,

---

(Toronto: University of Toronto Press, 2018); and taking the argument one step further in a sinological legal context see Norman Ho, 'Literature as Law? The Confucian Classics as Ultimate Sources of Law in Traditional China' (2019) 31(2) *Law and Literature* 173 who at 174 'proposes a different way of thinking about the interaction between law and literature in the Chinese context – literature *as* law, that is, the use of what are considered literary texts as sources of law for judicial decision-making'. I offer here the inverse of this formulation but I am confucious that they meet at their extremes.

5 I am borrowing here somewhat freely from Anne Genovese and Shaun McVeigh (2015) 'Nineteen eighty three: a jurisographic report on *Commonwealth v Tasmania*' (2015) 24(1) *Griffith Law Review* 68; and expounded most positively in Marett Leiboff, *Towards a Theatrical Jurisprudence* (London: Routledge, 2020).

while the French tradition (*mos gallicus*) tends to historicise. The English tradition (*mos britannicus*), as will be elaborated subsequently, is fond of myth, of Druidic origins, Biblical citations and an antiquity that reaches back to nature herself. The *mos americanus* is marked by the prevalence of policy and politics over law.[6] Each tradition tells its own story in its own rhetorical form, with its specific images and imaginal intendments. Law may seek to hide its performance, the political and theatrical character of its interventions, behind the black letters of the legal text but it takes only a cursory scrutiny of that typography, of those letters missive and familiar, to perceive the expansively figurative and diversely performative quality of such inventions. To think is to imagine, and the jurisliterary perspective upon legal expression is to approach the diversity of juristic forms, be they theoretical, educational, institutional, judicial or legislative, from the perspective of their literary and aesthetic qualities, situated in their historical and geographical context and place. This is really to ask how well the text or other performance, be it gestural, oratorical, visual, filmic, theatrical, plays its role and achieves its end. This is also to say that an aesthetic criterion is relevant to and matters for the thinking of law. The narrative of both code and case has to persuade and attach its auditors and readers while expressing the mood of its time and place. There is so much to hear in jurisliterature that it would be quite wrong to reduce it to a singular method or unique genre.

The starting point is an old antagonism. As Justinian formulates it in the opening to his educational text, the *Institutes*, he has compiled the laws from the constitutions of the emperors and the 'enormous volumes of the old jurisprudence' to ease the path of youth passionate for law (*juventus cupida legum*): 'you may start studying the law, not from what the ancient jurists said (*antiquae iuris fabulae*), but from your splendid emperor, and you may hear and learn nothing that is

---

6 On the *mos hispanicus*, see Susan Byrne, *Law and History in Cervantes'* Don Quixote (Toronto: Toronto U.P., 2012); and Bradin Cormack, *A Power to Do Justice: Jurisdiction, English Literature, and the Rise of Common Law, 1509–1625* (Chicago: Chicago U. P., 2007) on the jurisdiction of the literary within the *mos britannicus*; and explicitly on the *mos britannicus*, see Peter Goodrich, 'Intellection and Indiscipline' (2009) 36 *Journal of Law and Society* 460. Donald Kelley, *The Human Measure: Social Thought in the Western Legal Tradition* (Cambridge, MA: Harvard U.P., 1990) 187–209, provides a useful overview of the various national traditions with especial emphasis upon the *mos gallicus*. On the *mos americanus*, see Goodrich, 'Who are We?' in Desautels-Stein and Tomlins (eds), *Searching for Contemporary Legal Thought* (Cambridge: Cambridge University Press, 2017) at 43.

not useful or is out of place, but only the actual substance of the law'.[7] Two things are of interest in this foundational passage. First, the desire that underpins and drives the study of law. Affect is necessarily a part of learning, of understanding and interpreting the substance of law. There is desire and drive from the moment of first formal contact with the pedagogy of legality. Second, a significant part of the substantive law is comprised of *fabulae*, stories, plays, fabrications, images and fictions. The opening remark to the *Institutes* does not exclude these narratives, the old opinions and responses of the jurisconsults of early Rome, but rather tries to tame them in the form of a compilation that will order and reduce them in number. The old legal stories, as David Pugsley usefully elaborates, are tacked on to the end of Book 50 of the *Digest* under the heading 'Diverse Rules of Ancient Law' – *De diversis regulis iuris antiqui*.[8]

Affect and narrative are thus at the root of the early tradition and essential elements in teaching lusting youth the figures of law. Fabulation is jurisprudence, it is legislation, the jurispoetic activity of formulating the rules of law, of inventing the summaries and glosses, interpretations and possibilities of the legal tradition. There is also, in this working and reworking of the tradition both fabulation and legislation, fiction and rule, lightness and gravamen.[9] Throughout the genre of institutional expressions we witness a mode of what was termed *serio-ludere*, of play and seriousness, of serious playfulness. *Jus* and *jeu* are a letter apart, while as Judge Darling points out in his *Scintillae iuris*, borrowing from Horace, *jus* and *au jus*, law and sauce, are rather directly connected.[10] Legal elegance, felicity of formulation, involves the play of words and conjuring of thematic analogies, metaphor and matterphor, parsing

---

7 *Institutes* 1.4

8 David Pugsley, 'Justinian's Welcome to the Constantinople Law School' (2018) 24(1) *Fundamina* 57. He also cites usefully to Cujas, whose gloss on this point is *antiquorum iuris auctorum responsa* – the responses of the antique Roman legal authors. Suggesting even more strongly the creative character of this authorship.

9 Teissier-Ensminger, *Fabuleuse juridicité*, at 815, commenting that a principal theme of juris-literary works is that of 'historical retrospect, or better, under the flag of restitution, that of reconstruction of an undying odyssey, that of the beauty, both conceptual and formal, of legality.' This leads also, in her view, to the revivification of the ancient and harmonious fusion of law and speaking well or beautiful language. The theme is an important one in Richard Weisberg, *Poethics and Other Strategies of Law and Literature* (New York: Columbia University Press, 1992), especially chapter 1.

10 Charles J. Darling, *Scintillae juris* (London: Stevens and Haynes, 1889) preface: '*Est operae pretium duplicis pernoscere juris naturam*: says Horace. I believe he wrote thus concerning soup, but his remark applies very well to the kind of *jus* served out in our Courts of Law.'

and punning, malapropisms and other symptomatic materializations. There is a lengthy tradition, as Justinian implicitly recognizes, of erudite and imaginative elaborations of the comedy of law as a mode of introduction to the discipline and as a form of situating the work of the jurist – the jurispoet – within the corporation of disciplines and the play of laws. Poems, dramas, revels, dialogues, satires, picture books (*emblemata*), prefaces, discursive divagations of all sorts enact the imaginative life of the legal mind over the long term of the tradition.

The jurisliterary is a mobile and active category, a somewhat anarchic medley of approaches that seek to revivify and transform the juristic inheritance while sharing in the ludic yet lawful desire to invent imaginary solutions to hypothetical future conflicts. There is something of the pataphysician in the work of the best jurists. Recollect that pataphysics begins in a law suit and that the text is inaugurated by a summons. It is defined by Jarry as a science that 'examines the laws governing exceptions and . . . explain[s] the universe supplementary to this one'. In seeking to govern future acts, in stretching to encompass what has not and may never happen, the juristic drive is fuelled by affect and apprehension, by imaginings of events still to occur, informed by impossible predictions of the not yet. Invention, phantasms of futureity, laughter, despair, snoutfigs. In Jarry's words, 'I am bringing along some beings who have managed to escape your Law and your Justice between the lines of my seized volumes.'[11] It is in this sense that jurisliterature partakes in and contributes to the tradition of legal fiction, of studiously invented facts, theoretical 'as ifs' which place nebulous spokes upon the vaporous wheels of the unwritten constitution.

Jurisliterature conceived as being also a literary enterprise, a science of imaginary solutions, or in Daumal's definition, an application of the rules of objectivity to absences.[12] The approach to law via literary concepts involves an expansion and transfiguration of the legal tradition, allowing a place not only for multiple interdisciplinary conjunctions, but also for the enigmas, paradoxes and weird juxtapositions that laughter and law, comedy and manners, enthusiasm and boredom engender. It is this sense of magnificence and absurdity, the coexistence of invention and confinement, of future past, that permeates

---

11 Alfred Jarry, *Exploits and Opinions of Dr Faustroll, Pataphysician: A Neo Scientific-Novel* (Boston: Exact Change, 1996) respectively at 21, and 16–17.
12 René Daumal, 'The Pataphysics of Ghosts', in Daumal, *Pataphysical Essays* (Cambridge MA: Wakefield Press, 2012) at 91.

the wilder works of jurisliterature, the poetical sermons, the courts of love, mock trials, revels, the parallels of law and clothes, jurisprudence and poetry, musical judgments in minstrel run forums, curious customs, *facetiae*, all of which, in their elaboration and at their extreme allow for bursts of laughter as an antidote to the dust of filing cabinets and the smoke of pure law.

A final prolegomenal point. For those addicted to fingerposts and committed to road maps. Chapter 1, 'The Republic of Lawyers', begins the quest for a properly expansive account of jurisliterature by reviewing the classical tradition, from Greece to Rome to the Renaissance and early modern period. Jurists of many ilks and eras, penned a vast array of didactic, introductory and interpretative works, enchiridia, a panoply of poetic jurisprudences, laws of affect, fictions of a most just earth – *justissima tellus*. In this vein, Plato defines law as the best poetry, the lyric that deserves to survive, while the Roman tradition developed a concept of legal elegance and oratorical forensic felicity, discourses of juristic passion. For the Renaissance the recuperation and extension of the great imaginative works of the legal past, the expansion of the arts of law (*bonae artes*) was always the goal of the jurists' desire. The poetics of law builds a creative concept of an embodied and performative literature of law's heterotopic spaces, its reveries of beauty and perfection, both intellective and aesthetic. The *Republic of Lawyers*, an exemplary work that visits the island of jurisprudence to meet the great jurists of the past, is the model for an historical account of the great creative figures, the poets and geniuses of the legal tradition.[13]

Chapter 2, 'The Discipline of Law', looks to the long term of legal style and the traditional literary practices of lawyers and judges. The history of law is of a sacral profession, of temples of justice and tablets of stone, tables of commandments, of speech directed to posterity, impermeable and resistant to change. Legal discourse is in considerable measure the chatter of stones, the patina of the permanent, an argot not used in everyday life, and the first step of a jurisliterary accounting of the tradition is to address its use of Biblical and other scriptural and dogmatic sources. The *mos britannicus* is one that relies to a considerable extent upon a mythology of divine, natural and Druidic roots of the tradition, ley lines as law lines, and expressly adopts the fictions of time out of mind or immemorial – the *auctoritates poetarum* – as sources of an

---

[13] Giuseppe Aurelio di Gennaro, *Respublica jurisconsultorum* (1731), and in translation, *La République des jurisconsultes* (Paris: Lyon, 1768).

esoteric, unwritten, oral and imagistic legality. This leads in Chapter 3 to the analysis of legal allegory in recognition of the extensive role of the fictive and literary as sources of law. *Allegoresis*, the juridical practice of interpreting law as allegory, as the expanded elaboration of the 'as if' or narrative of acts and behaviours, rules and judgments, depends upon the invention of facts and rules for novel circumstances. Where law runs out, which is to say whenever a new situation, be it a new person, a new fact, a new event, is genuinely encountered, then literature will become a source of law. The Judge will reach for the Bible, Shakespeare, the poets, Melville, matterphor, metaphor, malapropisms, film and art to invent their judgment and relay their affects as well as their reasons.

Chapter 4, 'Legal Imaginations', expands the scope and scopic range of jurisliterature to include new media and the visual. The era of the exclusion of photographs, films and other images from the courts is over, and cameras intrude, judges insert pictures in judgments, social media and microblogging impact and influence the practice of lawyers, as also the performances, the reasoning and the decisions of the courts. The visual culture of law is now on display both inside and outside of courts and their judgments. The imagery of law, the whole gamut of theatrical and filmic dimensions of juridical and juristic performances, from the architecture of the courthouses, to the costumes of the players, the portraiture, thrones and regalia of law's formal sites and various parliaments, the podia and lecterns of the schoolroom are all now visible in the images that manifest in public spaces and in the depictions of law that advocates and judges use.

In Chapter 5, 'Transitions', the full scope and the excitement of the jurisliterary reaches its crescendo in the contemporary neo-materialist and *trans* discourses evident in a culture of accelerating change. The legal imagination returns to the body, to affect, performance and the grounds of daily life. New materialism connects culture and law to the spaces, atmospheres, and corporeal affects through which it is performed. The old concept of 'laws of the land' – *leges terrae* – gains novel expression in a return to *justissima tellus*, the Latin term for a most just earth. The materiality of law, its transhuman qualities and earthbound expressions unsettle the dogmatic and positivistic complacencies of inherited legalisms by recognizing that earth and law, atmosphere and affect are in constant motion, mobile and transforming. Nothing is still; all is quick. This allows for the reconstruction of the jurisprudence of the first great modern trans lawyer, the German

Supreme Court Judge Daniel Paul Schreber who stepped down from the bench because he believed he was becoming a woman. He nailed his flag, as he put it, to the feminine and suffered the torture and invention of changing gender at the end of the nineteenth century. What has been too little considered is the novel and trans character of his choice of gender, of Miss Schreber's mobile and mutating body, the screams of a jurist confined, immobilized in a binary and static conception of sex.

Schreber escaped, we still read hir, and their jurisprudence was of connection, corporeality and the earthly quality of any meaningful matter and law.[14] She got away, he suffered, but they live on as part of the collectivity of intellection, the long line of great figures of imaginative jurists, the community of lovers of the potentiality of legality, the vast host of those who remained alive by means of remaining in constant motion – *perpetuum mobile*. Thought never sleeps, so Freud taught us, and that is because the body, like the earth that produced it, is ever mutating, transforming, moving. Transitional jurisprudence imagines new sexes, plural genders, the absence of any need to choose any one identity or thought. That leads finally to the 'Epilogue', the invocation and expression of the pataphysics, the unknown, at the heart of law. Jurisliterature too is a science of imaginary solutions, a discourse on holes, an aesthetic of opportunities, the lasting laughter of becoming who we are.

---

14 For an elaboration of Schreber's jurisprudence, see Peter Goodrich, *Schreber's Law: Jurisprudence and Judgment in Transition* (Edinburgh: Edinburgh University Press, 2019).

1 The republic of lawyers

The literary character and frequently esoteric quality of legal expression can be exemplified dynamically by a cryptogram. In the case of *Baigent v Random House*, the publishers of the best-selling novel, *The Da Vinci Code* were sued for copyright infringement. Two of the three authors of an earlier work of historical conjecture, the literary faction *The Holy Blood and The Holy Grail*, claimed that the later work had purloined its central theme from their book. Chancery Judge Peter Smith had to read and compare the two works and determine first whether the theme of *Holy Blood* was original and so meriting protection, and second whether, if found to be original, it had been substantially infringed.[1] In an extended exercise of jurisliterary criticism, the Judge determined that the claimant's work lacked any sufficiently discernible structure to be infringed and that there had been no relocation of its actual words, and so dismissed the suit. In doing so, the Judge distinguished law from literature, stating in the mode of denial, that 'a judgment is not a work of fiction (I hope) nor is it a piece of conjectural fact'.[2] The observation, a species of oratorical conclusion, comes at the very end of the judgment, under the heading 'Other Matters', as a peroration and is supported only by the further methodological aperçu that '[a] judge distils the facts and determines those facts which he concludes are necessary to enable him to come to a decision in the case. That is what I have attempted to do'.

While the Judge is conscious of the duty to determine, to end the dispute, the denial of the creative character of deciding the case, of inventing a conclusion is intriguing and symptomatic, or in the older language it is heavily rhetorical. The comparison of the faction and the fiction together with relevant law spans a judgment of over 360 paragraphs, a not insubstantial literary effort in the mode of the 'as if', namely that of hypothesis, invention, rhetorical turns, sensibility

---

[1] *Baigent v Random House Group Ltd* [2006] EWHC 719.
[2] *Baigent* at para. 358.

and impression. Although the Judge accepts that *The Da Vinci Code* copied language from the earlier work, this was neither substantial nor significant and so the case is to be decided on the question of 'non-textual infringement', an abstract question of the appropriation of the structure, architecture, themes, labour and skill of the author of the copyrighted text. Again, the Judge is convinced that many of the central themes of the later work are drawn from the earlier book but after careful reading, research and extensive cross-examination at trial, the similarities are insufficient, not least because the earlier text lacks any coherent structure or architecture of themes. Upon examination indeed as to the organizational form of their narrative 'the claimants' skeleton fell away leaving in my view a complete denouement with a lame chronological order'.

It is evidently difficult to deny the literary quality of a decision that compares two works of fiction according to the originality of the copied work, the independence of skill and labour in its composition and themes, architecture and realization, and then the substantial quality of the borrowing, the degree of reliance. It is expressly a question of forming a 'picture' of the two works, of gaining 'an impression', of 'a feeling', of looking for 'fingerprints', or in the more general language of Blackstone, 'the Judges of the Court upon testimony of their own senses, shall decide the point'.[3] Judge Peter Smith may state the work of comparison in the case 'is not ... an exercise in literary criticism of either book', but the analysis expresses virulent negative views of the earlier work, while also lauding the successful novel and its formal inventions, including the novelty of an academic lecture as an innovative genre in a thriller, and approbative comments upon the use of anagrams and codes, as well as appreciating 'the special attractiveness' of Brown's 'well-received thriller'.[4] It is hardly even necessary to point to the *in vivo* apprehensions of trial, that Dan Brown 'wriggled in the witness box', that his wife and researcher Blythe Brown's refusal to testify was unsatisfactory and indicative that she would not support her husband's assertions as to sources. Baigent is lambasted as something more than 'a poor witness', as 'unconvincing', as asserting 'wild evidence', as ignorant and incredible, so much so that his motives are

---

3 Sir William Blackstone, *Commentaries on the Laws of England* [1767–8] (Oxford: Oxford University Press, 2016) vol. 1 at 218.

4 *Baigent* at para. 164. The comment on the academic lecture is at para. 61. The comment on the special attractiveness of the novel is at para. 270.

impugned: 'Why do the claimants bring the claim I conjecture? . . . They may be disappointed that Mr Brown has done so well . . .'[5]

Clearly the Judge has been too laconic. The judgment is stuffed with conjectures, both express and implied, and it is suffused with fiction. Contrary to the general expression, adverted to above, that it is 'not a work of fiction (I hope)', it is evident that the Judge's work, the lengthy, lovingly penned and exquisitely detailed text that determines the outcome is not only about fiction, full of borrowed fiction, but is itself both rhetorically inventive, and distinctive in style. More than that, as if to crown the determination as a literary work in its own right, the Judge inserts a cryptogram, legally an enigma, into his judgment.[6] The approved judgment famously contains an encrypted message. Interspersed in the text were italicized letters, in bold font. When excised and combined, the letters made the following statement: 'Smithy Code. Jackie Fisher, who are you? Dreadnought.' It transpires that not only is the judgment a work of fiction, a creative exercise incorporating a remarkably novel figurative device, but it also and irrefragably disproves the Judge's subsequent and self-effacing remark, that the judgment, the 'distillation . . . of the facts', is 'unlike literary works of the type featured in the case'.[7] This statement can be understood in two ways. It specifies that a judgment is not a literary fiction and so perhaps limits the denial of the fictive to the genre of literature. In this sense, legal fiction is a distinct genre of the fictive, a species of creative writing that is forced for institutional reasons to appear distinct from, different to and a refinement of other creative genres and works of imagination, while remaining resolutely and necessarily a creative act and poetic exercise of expression.

Judge Smith's cryptogram is exceptional and finely indicative in a second and stronger sense. It sits on the cusp of a new genre of juristic writing and of judicial determination which both recognizes affect and endeavours to be more transparent in expressing the affective and perceptual sources of judgment. The enigmatic cryptogram is ironically the expression of the Judge's engagement with the literary works subject to scrutiny, an indication of his enthusiasm, and so also of the desire that triggers the decision. In proleptic alignment with the

---

[5] *Baigent* at para. 268.
[6] For discussion of this aspect of the case, see P. Goodrich, 'Legal Enigmas: Antonio de Nebrija, *The Da Vinci Code* and the Emendation of Law' (2010) *Oxford J. Legal Studies* 71.
[7] *Baigent* at para. 358.

new materialism in jurisprudence, the judicial text enacts an active sense of law as a performance, as rhythm and movement of bodies in spaces, as atmosphere and sensibility expressed allegorically and in enigmatic codes that act as an allure for both Judge and reader alike. The exorbitant sales of *The Da Vinci Code* say as much, but it takes the creativity and jurisliterary brilliance of the Judge to formulate this as a novel mode of legal expression, and at the cost of reprimand by the Court of Appeal.

The embedded, coded statement provides a figure of invention and a window on the motive of decision. It is in its openness to novelty, in its caress of history and the poetics of jurisprudence that the judgment entertains and prefigures new themes of affect, perception, collective intellection, inscription, painting words, and the imaginal sensibilities of law's expanding visual culture. The invention of the cryptogram provides, intentionally or otherwise, an image of the decisional process. The Judge is also an aggregation of atoms, a maelstrom of molecules, a concatenation of cells, a fulmination of flesh, vibrating, recombining, palpitating, an opening and closing of pores that smell and sense, see and hear, feel and judge. It is that real yet phantasmatic interior of Judge and judgment that the cryptogram beautifully yet elliptically reveals at the level of imagining judgment. More prosaically, because for lawyers prose is our immediate medium, the encryption provides an image of the ground of judgment, of its foundation in imagination. The Judge is seeking to communicate, reaching out for dialogue, providing a clue, and when, rather depressingly none of the very highly paid advocates noticed the encryption, Smith J. went to some lengths to notify a journalist of its existence.

An enigma is classically a reference to a forgotten source, and so for purposes of completion, the encryption references the theft of the plans for a new design of naval battleship. The invention of the design was by the Italian architect Vittorio Cunniberti, but it was Jackie Fisher who took the plans and built the Dreadnought, which became for a while the pre-eminent warship on the high seas. The actualization of the plans was the key to success and the Dreadnought was both huge in guns and a dominating presence. The point is that Jackie Fisher is to Cunniberti what Dan Brown is to Baigent and Leigh. *The Da Vinci Code* is to the *The Holy Blood and The Holy Grail* what Dreadnought was to the lesser gunned ships that preceded it. The theft of naval drawings and latterly the infringement of copyright pale into insignificance when compared to the building of the Dreadnought by Jackie

Fisher and the huge success of the novel by Dan Brown. In the last instance, the Judge decides poetically, in favour of fiction, preferring the thriller to the faction, the best seller to the mediocre relay of the prior promulgation, the full-bodied opus to the vanishing skeleton, the confused falling away of an innovative but incoherent work.

The Republic of Letters and the Republic of Lawyers are one and the same, single and several in their imbrications. The diversity of literary genres does not preclude that of law but rather is enmeshed and indissolubly in dialogue with that of the jurist. The *Da Vinci* case judgment admirably evinces the jurisliterary, a term I am myself misappropriating from the monumentally erudite study, *Fabuleuse juridicité*, which translates best as *Fabricating Legality*, a study of the aesthetics of law.[8] The juridical has its origin – its own originality – in the formulae and fabulations of the poet or, as one early lawyer puts it, humans play games and tell tales.[9] Poetry, has its roots in *poiesis* meaning creation, fabrication and fabulation, as well as the more specific harmonies of sound, incantation, melody and rhythm of speech, that were deemed to have generated the first law. Poetics is the mode of instituting the bonds of the social and the eloquence of community that make collective cohabitation possible. Long before the social contract there is the theory – mythology, theosophy, or fabulation – that it is poetry, the zodiac of wit taking the rhyming form of verse, that founds the Republic of Lawyers.[10] The tradition goes back to the Greek philosopher Pythagoras who believed musical harmony was the primary bond of the socius and that where conflict broke out, playing a tune was the best and most eloquent form of dissipating the hostile animus and so resolving the conflict. Judge Peter Smith's witty and instructive cryptogram is thus a form of reviving an earlier juristic tradition of legal poetics in which it is the soothing and soothsaying character of the judicial remedy, the appositeness of the juristic intervention to the occasion, that makes for an art of justice defined most boldly by eloquence of

---

8 Anne Teissier-Enmsminger, *Fabuleuse juridicité. Sur la littérarisation des genres juridiques* (Paris: Garnier, 2015) at 8–10 distinguishing fiction focused upon law from jurisliterature which is comprised in her definition primarily by literary, which is to say imaginative introductions to law by jurists or more broadly didactic literary accounts of law produced by lawyers.
9 Jan-Luis Vives, *Aedes legum* [1520] (Leipzig: Teubner, 1984 edn) – *homo ipse ludus et fabula est*. The theme of *homo ludens*, is most famously taken up in Johan Huizinga, *Homo ludens: A Study of the Play Element in Culture* (Boston: Beacon Press, 1971) where law as play, as a game, is analysed in detail.
10 The Zodiack of wit comes from Philip Sidney, *An Apologie for Poetrie* [1595] (Oxford: Clarendon Press, 1907) at 8.

expression and elegance of adumbration. The classical authority of the poets (*auctoritates poetarum*), the harmonies introduced by the bards – jongleurs, troubadours, lovers, clowns, comediennes and fools – have a foundational role to play as unacknowledged inventors of the juridical and as the earliest practitioners of dispute resolution in peaceful forms. As Vico puts it:

> Ancient jurisprudence was throughout poetic. By its fictions what had happened was taken as not having happened; those not yet born as already born; the living as dead ... It introduced innumerable ... *iura imaginaria*, rights invented by imagination. It rested its entire reputation on inventing such fables as might preserve the gravity of the laws and do justice to the facts.[11]

When in legal argot a judge says that an argument sounds, we might even expand the expression and say that here the law rhymes, it sings, it is just. These are what the Greeks termed *nomes*, chanted laws, and the early orators called necessary songs – *carminem necessarium*.[12]

First point, *prima regula*, the law of poetry and the poetry of law are born singly and severally in the same vein, to a common purpose and as differing but both foundational genres of our being together. These are golden chains, social wedlock, the tools of a sensibility of law, and sign posts of an art of justice that includes music, verse, narrative, imagery and overall a persuasive aesthetic of being in common. The argument, perhaps surprisingly to contemporary disciplinary norms, goes back to Plato, that great critic of cacophonic music, weak verse, poor rhetoric and wooden theatrics. It is in the *Laws* that he sets out his mature and most complete theory of the best legislator or perfect jurist. It is the philosophy and ethics of education, propaedeutics, that provides the training and model for formation of the legislator and so for the best laws. The resources for the good legislator are medicine and poetry, or as Teissier-Ensminger puts it, a double medicine, corporeal and affective, it being the task of the good legislator to maintain the health and well-being of body and soul, the polity and its denizens.[13] Medicine

---

11 Giambattista Vico, *The New Science* [1744] (Ithaca: Cornell University Press, 1984) at 390.
12 The sources go back to the Greeks and citations are usually to Homer and to a lesser extent Plato and Plutarch. The genealogy of the conjunction are usefully adumbrated in a remarkable work by the French Renaissance legal humanist Jean Broé, *Parallela poesis et iurisprudentiæ* (Paris, 1664) where the theme and sources are lengthily elaborated. For a recent and erudite study, see Valérie Hayaert, 'The Versification of Legal Codes', in Subha Mukherji (ed.), *Law and Poetry* (London: Palgrave, 2021).
13 *Fabuleuse juridicité* at 28–36.

will cure the ills of the social body, while poetry, as also the best music, dance, song and play will ensure attachment to law and harmony of emotions. It is the poet and the poetico-musical paradigm that are given the greatest attention by the legislator and form the basis of good laws, an art of justice that remodels wounded affects and teaches best practices. In this Platonic formulation it is precisely the emotional and ethical practices of the subject, the interior machinations that through the instructions of the poet, are to be orchestrated and attached to the good, defined as individual and social health.

Humans are for Plato 'the plaything of God', aspirants to an ideal that is accessible through nature and taught by the 'divine' poets. It is this foundational role of the poet that lies at the heart of the *Laws* conceived as human enactments of higher causes, of laws painted in imitation of nature. Although the dialogue takes a frequently antinomic form, opposing war to law, it tracks a median path and subtly advocates friendship and peace, purge and poetry as the path to social well-being. The old Athenian, the principal protagonist of the dialogue, early in the first Book, thus derides the Spartan warrior who says: 'I sing not, I care not, about any man . . . if he be not at all times a brave warrior.'[14] The point, ironically, is to praise loyalty, meaning commitment to kin and friends, country and cause as the ethical grounds of attachment. The higher law is virtue, taught by the poets to the legislator in the order of justice, temperance and wisdom, aimed against pain and ultimately at 'making those that use them happy'.

The key role of poetry is reiterated through praise of named poets and their role in educating the legislator of the laws. This leads in the second Book to a lengthy praise of the legislative use of dance and song: 'But what I am telling you about music is true and deserving of consideration, because showing that a lawgiver may institute melodies which have a natural truth and correctness without any fear of failure', and 'if a person can only find in any way the natural melodies, he may confidently embody them in a fixed and legal form.'[15] Chants, it is later argued, were invented to enchant, and so to put harmony in the soul. It is this theme of persuasion, and social attachment that culminates in Book 7 in the remarkable recognition that theatre and poetry at their best are the essence of law: 'You are poets and we are poets,

---

14 Plato, *Laws*, in *The Collected Dialogues* (Princeton: Princeton University Press, 1962) Bk 1 at 644 d–e (Athenian).
15 *Laws*, Bk II at 657 b–c.

both makers of the same strains, rivals and antagonists in the noblest of dramas, which true law can alone perfect.' It is desire for the best, which is the most harmonious and effective lesson of the poets, as also the most skilled theatre and dance, that the legislator seeks for the good of the social whole:

> Wherefore, O ye sons and scions of the softer Muses, first of all show your songs to the magistrates, and let them compare them with our own, and if they are the same or better we will give you a chorus; but if not, then, my friends, we cannot. Let these, then, be the customs ordained by law about all dances and the teaching of them.[16]

A social body that sings together, incants together, is one that is in tune with common purposes and their affective bonds. As Aristotle later puts it in the *Ethics*, the good legislator pays more attention to friendship than to law, meaning in this context that social harmony, the poetics of relationship, bind the polity, preceding and where successful precluding the need for medical and surgical incisions in the social body. It is the poetry of law that persuades and binds without need for force and arms, punishment and excommunication.

If we recall that the poets teach the legislator it follows that this didactic role is one of opening the subject, raising the penthouse lids of the eyes to see the harmony of the social and the laws of its bonds. In other words, the thesis is that we come to law through poetry and the teachings of the great poets, whose discourse in Plato and in much of later jurisprudence takes the form of a dialogue of instruction. This is in part because the first addressee of legal instruction is the child, and an education in virtue and justice, teaching 'how rightly to rule, and how to obey . . . is the first and fairest thing that the best of men can ever have'.[17] In the early institutional writings, the neophyte, in the old books *juventus cupida legum*, youth eager for law, is the initial audience, the subject to be inducted into the first law books, variously termed enchiridion, parergon, direction or preparative. These works are literary overtures, prefaces, preludes, apertures and openings.[18] What is at issue in the poetic texts and in introductory 'institutional' writings is precisely entry into the discipline, a first knowledge per-

---

16 *Laws*, Bk VII at 846 d–e. Kenji Yoshino, 'The City and the Poet' (2005) 114 *Yale L.J.* 1835, 1858–60, also usefully highlights this passage.
17 *Laws*, Bk 1.
18 The expression comes from Justinian's *Institutes* (London: Duckworth, 1984 edn) *proemium*.

formed in the alluring and figurative language, in the imagery and tones, of the dialogic. Dialogue is democratic, diverse and most famously for the Russian literary theorist Bakhtin, it is carnivalesque, festive and comedic, as well as persuasive and combative, engaged and plural.[19] The second point is thus that the dialogic form of Plato's discourse on the *Laws* has a poignant pedagogic purpose and figurative significance that recurs throughout the later juristic tradition. In the dialogue of the *Laws* the old Athenian plays the part of the pedagogue, and is concerned primarily with establishing through debate the legal structures that will direct legislation and law interpreters in future cases. The form of the dialogue indicates in an express form the communicative and performative character of exchange of ideas and the active modes of passing on wisdom, knowledge and in our case law.

The dialogic form is repeated throughout the juristic tradition and most particularly in foundational humanistic legal texts, the key institutional writings that in the common law tradition, for example, would include Sir John Fortescue's *Praise of the Laws of England*, a dialogue of instruction between the Chancellor and the Prince; and Christopher St Germain's *Doctor and Student*, an exchange between a canon lawyer and a common lawyer.[20] There are myriad other examples of such dialogues in the foundational eras of early modern common law and its constitutive writings, although Thomas Starkey's mid-fifteenth century *Dialogue between Reginald Pole and Thomas Lupset* is as good an example as any of the recourse to the genre of dialogue when issues of the structure or frame of law are in question. For Starkey the issue of the day was the politically explosive one of whether England should abandon the polylingual, particularistic, case-based and unwritten or 'illiterate' Anglican common law in favour of the written reason of Roman law and the civilian tradition, which could plausibly be argued to be older, more rational, and in comity with the other European nations. The dialogic form is foundational. It takes up a conversation and expressly addresses the figure – the *prosopopoeia* or personification – of other positions and different perspectives. Dialogue acknowledges the multiplicity of community and the plurality of the polity and, as Bakhtin so ably argues, it represents in generic form the heteroglossia

---

19 Mikhail Bakhtin, *The Dialogic Imagination* (Austin: Texas University Press, 1981); Desmond Manderson, *Kangaroo Courts and the Rule of Law* (London: Routledge, 2012); Julien Extabe, 'Bakhtin on Language: An Assault on Legal Positivism' (ms forthcoming).
20 Thomas Starkey, *A Dialogue between Reginald Pole and Thomas Lupset* [1535] (London: Chatto and Windus, 1945).

of all discursive practice, including and especially contentiously that of law. This is because 'no language is unitary', no word is original or free of context, history and purpose, but rather carries a history of usage with it, including that of the persons, occasions and events of utterance across (*dia*) which speech (*logos*) occurs.

That foundational texts take the form of dialogue is a healthy reminder of the cut that inaugurates, the severing of the umbilical chord of the past that marks the fiction of origin or of constitution as a pure beginning. There is necessarily a before, a cacophony of other voices, tones, and discursive utterances that are sidelined, excluded and often suppressed in the event of founding an institution, tradition or a constitution. Focus upon the dialogic genre and the dialogism of practice is to direct critical attention onto the social and political genealogy of legal discourse. It is devised in dialogue and often in the tension and agonism of conflict. It is authored by institutional office holders in specific times and places, in response to subjects and discourses, events and practices, law suits and other conflicts to which and to whom it replies. The dialogic genre of foundational discourses exhibits the openness of the text both to its past and to its auditors, lectors and variable recipients. The foundational character of the dialogue also has a further function, which is that of placing the discourse within the community of disciplines which form the institutional framework of the specific tradition, collects and collections of writings and practices, which law seeks to frame and administer. Just as no word is virginal or alone but carries a history of usage, of intonations and interactions with it, so the discipline of law, the specific mode of teaching law within a particular jurisdiction, is also housed within a set of institutions and a collection of disciplines. The common law tradition, our prime example in this work, belongs firmly within the European, Western body of law and founds itself in relation to and interaction with other legal authorities, historically Roman and Canon law, and then theology, philosophy, philology, rhetoric, and history as the disciplinary progenitors of *mos britannicus iuris docendi*, or in translation, the Anglican manner of teaching law, in comparison to the Italian, Gallic, and Hispanic genres of the Western legal inheritance of Roman law. A legal tradition, as a genre of literature, is a complex and colourful formation of multiple conversations, sites of intersection and diffraction that create the specific mode of discourse and the peculiarities of the jurisdiction. These will be returned to and analysed later; it is for present purposes the commonalities, intersections, habitudes and shared relays and topics of the disciplines that foundational dialogue as a genre promotes that will be our focus.

Disciplines are to be understood as imaginal and corporeal, as collectivities of thought carried by specific institutional bodies, varied officeholders, and the sensibilities of those who inhabit such juridical locations. One facet is that a discipline is already in a nascent or inchoate form a legal category, something framed and ordered by the foundational distribution of knowledge practices and, as the root of the word in the figure of the disciple suggests, it follows upon an extant structure, the family of disciplines that is established, initially at least, by theology as the relay of divine decree. There is no discipline of law without the religious inculcation of the clerics, the early scriptoria or writing workshops that copied texts and authorized publications by pontifical and then later royal decree. The discipline of philology would recover and relay the texts of the tradition, while linguistics and literary criticism, hermeneutics and rhetoric would teach the jurist how to interpret and apply the codified rules or the records of judgment. A community of disciplines is implicit in the definition, demarcation and practice of law. It is a point that can be made in relatively recent form by reference to a foundational dialogue that sought to elaborate in interactive mode the sense and purpose of critique and critical legal studies (CLS) in the USA. Here, in 1984, it is not Chancellor and Prince, nor Doctor of Canon Law and Student of Common Law who are the figures, but two law professors who had been pivotal in the development of the CLS movement.

The dialogue begins, because it is intrinsic to the form, with an opening, a discussion in the broadest of metaphysical and philosophical formulations of the foundational question of what constitutes the project, program, vision or goal of CLS. The issue which could be interpreted abstractly as one of birth and so of lineage, is rapidly transformed into much more visceral questions of experiences, relationships, events, and also of moods, feelings, friendships and fallings out. How do we know who we are, is the basic topic of the first part of the dialogue and this involves engaging both with the disciplinary sources of critical outlooks and practices, as also with the specific discussant in the dialogue. Experience and engagements, enthusiasms and affects rapidly emerge replete with evocations of 'love', 'friendship', 'yearnings', 'zap', jokes, music and laughter. The serious, as Plato notes in the *Laws*, cannot be understood without the laughable, and the comedy of the human is highly significant to understanding the lifeworld of the critical lawyer, as much as that of any other jurist.[21]

---

21 Peter Gabel and Duncan Kennedy, 'Roll Over Beethoven' (1984) 36 *Stanford Law Rev.* 1.

The dialogue is intimate and, in this instance, explicitly affective and relational. Bodies think and feel, move and change position both physically and metaphorically. Thus, for example, when seeking to resist an abstract theory of human nature that will frame practical activity, the response is: 'Well, that's a good idea – to undercut it the minute that it becomes frozen in the same way that rights discourse becomes frozen. The minute that it becomes frozen in a mood that corresponds to a "program".'[22] Better to joke, to play, to keep the movement mobile, put on music, stay honest to 'the inner reality', the spirit of freedom, the anarchic drive, the brouhaha of creativity. By the same token, more viscerally, the desire compelling the dialogue is that of building an immediate community of thought, one that is alive to body and affect, tone and feeling, including moments of conflict, anxiety, fear, worry and love. Thus at one point the response is 'Shut up a minute! I agree with you. Don't lock me in that way.' And then later, when Peter Gabel refers to the 'deeply trusting' mode of his friendship with Duncan Kennedy, he continues that 'it is always corroded by some degree of fear, anxiety, mistrust . . . the potential for being – whatever you say – 'reduced to misery by a friend's glance'.' And Duncan responds 'I'm feeling very anxious. I have no idea why. I feel nervous that we are in a box. We're being too discursive.'[23]

The immediate point is that the dialogue is a corporeal performance as well as being an abstract introduction to the project of Critical Legal Studies. Different languages engage and deliberate while the phenomenological and Marxist roots of the movement are elaborated and contested. Philosophical, literary, sociological and political sources are set out and the theoretical and imaginal spaces of the radical law professor are debated. Numerous distinct voices emerge; there are renunciations, denunciations, recantings, digressions, anecdotes, and multiple further flageolets and fripples throughout. What is striking and relevant to the humanist themes of legal poetics and jurisliterature is that the relationship of law to other disciplines, languages, traditions and jurisdictions is openly acknowledged and adumbrated as something that is important to both *dramatis personae* of the dialogue. Relationships matter, friendship is evident, networks, links, institutional ties, the imbrication of self and subject, person and discipline in a community of intellective and intergenerational sites and projects gains expression. Friendship, and I would add enmity, affection and hostility play important roles

---

22 'Roll Over' at 3.
23 'Roll Over' at 21.

or, in a recent neologism, are matterphorical.[24] Which friends matter, what ideas do we feel affection for, how is amity expressed in and for our community of intellect and passage of ideas? Amity and its affects, enmity and its ejections define group reproduction as much in academia and law as in other institutions, and dialogue, whether explicit, or in the exegetical form of lengthy side notes and references in early modern printed texts, and today in footnotes and now, more frequently asterisk and endnotes. All discourse is dialogue in the sense both of the philological history and communities of usage that words inevitably bear, as also in the discursive purposes and communities of reception that specific utterances invoke. The Republic of Lawyers is as bound to the social character of discourse and the community of disciplines as any other collectivity of utterances or users of a shared language.

The specific character and aesthetic quality of legal dialogue, the discursive formation of law, has historically taken a gargantuan and spectacular form. The founder of law, the great poet, is variously put forward in the figure of nature, God, sovereign, legislator, President, and populace. Their child and institution is variously depicted as a temple, a fortress, a castle, a shrine, a treasure chest so as to give a sense of the distinctiveness of law and project a quality of autonomy. The Republic of Lawyers aims to distinguish legality from other disciplines, to project separateness and authority, replete with an aura of divinity and permanence of expression. The oldest laws come as commandments carved on stone, inscriptions of the law on bronze tablet, as in the Roman Twelve Tables, lists of rules posted high on columns, as with the Greek Emperor Solon's laws, and then in the great compilation of the Emperor Justinian, the pandects or collection of all the laws in the *Corpus iuris civilis* that the Western legal tradition inherited, and that forms the basis of modern law in the Occident and beyond. The latter work is exemplary of the later tradition and indeed founds the Republic of Lawyers in its Christian form as servants of God and Emperor following in the footsteps of the early and greatest of Codes, the holy letters of governance, a sacral tradition slowly becoming a secular though not yet a profane social form.

---

24 Daniela Gandorfer, *Matterphorics: On the Laws of Theory* (forthcoming, Duke University Press). See also, on amity and enmity, Goodrich, *Skeletons of Amity: Lives Lived in Exodus from Law* (London: Routledge, 2021).

It is the special quality and distinctive character of legal institutions, their antiquity and permanence that gain greatest stress in the early modern tradition, in the histories and precedents that form the literary tradition of legality, the jurisliterature of our study. The question is what sort of literary form is that of law, what is the aesthetic of its diction, how is it to be read and re-read, interpreted and criticized. 'Religion and law', according to the English Renaissance lawyer William Fulbecke, 'do lie down together'.[25] For the Elizabethan antiquarian John Selden, it was Gods, 'the Samothes' that first brought law to the English and after that it was Druids and then Kings that relayed the axioms of legal dogma, the esoteric knowledge and language of the Anglican legal tradition under the sign of the two faced Roman divinity Janus, the emblem of common law.[26] For Sir Edward Coke and other early compilers and commentators of English law, the figure of legal discourse was that of a seamless tradition, embedded in time immemorial, coeval with the land, and passed in an unbroken lineage from an antiquity so ancient as to originate in nature and so also in immediate proximity to God. For the English, common law was older even than the laws of Greece and Rome and so formed a particular discourse and distinct jurisdiction carried in an argot that was peculiarly British. Although the early common lawyers might not have been quite so explicit, they would doubtless have agreed with Bishop Aylmer who boldly states in a work of Anglican dogma, that 'God is English'.[27]

The various European legal traditions all have their idiosyncracies and specificities as styles of jurisliterature and these were established in the Renaissance and early modern eras. The Italian mode of teaching law – *mos italicus iuris docendi* – associated most often with the German legal system, is one which prefers literalism, the direct authority and application of the Roman law. The French Renaissance lawyers broke away from that reception and tradition and favoured an historical approach, updating and modifying the Roman law of the *Corpus iuris* in light of the changed local and historical context of France – *mos gallicus iuris docendi*. The Spanish tradition, associated in large part with work of the legally trained author Cervantes, *mos hispanicus iuris docendi*, favoured literary accounts of local law, mixed with inherited Roman legal codes, to provide a more fictive account of the *Partides*

---

25 William Fulbecke, *Direction or Preparative for the Study of Law* (London: Clarke, 1599) at 33.
26 John Selden, *Jani Anglorum facies altera* (London: Society of Stationers, 1614).
27 Bishop Aylmer, *An Harborowe for Faithfull and Trewe Subjectes against the late blowne blaste* (Strasburg, 1559) at 36.

or written codes of the Iberian regions. English common law was aesthetically distinctive as well, and as adumbrated, for a more explicit recourse to mythology, to the esoteric and arcane figures of Druids and time immemorial, sources that were expressly 'beyond the memory of man' and so spectral, matters of spiritualism, ley lines, and of local divinities of the land, the *lex terrae* or tellurian and so supposedly natural, God given form of this particular poetic tradition of unwritten, law.

The Anglican juridical tradition, *mos britannicus iuris docendi*, to use the last example, shares its language and institutional forms, its semiotic relay and textual proclivities with the European tradition. Like all the different forms of transmission it seeks in literary form to establish a lineage of transmission which in the Anglican mode lacks any one Text. The castle of law, the tower of justice, the structure and institutions of the legal tradition are relayed in unbroken form by great men, *propositae*, who act, in the old spelling, as the presidents, and later precedents, of the insular tradition. Thus Sir Edward Coke starts the first volume of the *Institutes of the Laws of England*, of 1610, with an image of the Propositus, the great man, who stood at the helm of the English tradition, Sir Thomas Lyttleton, and an inscription of the genealogical tree, *arbor jurisdictionis*, to which he belonged.[28] The Republic of Lawyers is different and special is the first message of the legal literature and their offices require respect, their languages demand awe and obedience, their personnel belong to a tradition unsullied by common use and marked rather by a special if no longer expressly sacral character.

At the root of the tradition, in other words, is an image of distinctiveness, a depiction of a territory and place, which houses the great men of the jurisdiction and that is specifically legal in character. In the European tradition we find this form of legal literature most explicitly in accounts of an Island of Jurisprudence, law here being figured explicitly as an insular territory that has to be journeyed to in arduous forms. The four protagonists of the Italian jurisliterary fiction, *The Republic of Lawyers*, from which my chapter title is taken, embark upon a lengthy and difficult journey, an epic quest, to the Island of Jurisprudence, or in the technical language of law, of Jurisconsults. This species of pilgrimage to the intellectual atopia of law is a mission to the communal and enduring space of law as civility pitched against

---

28 Sir Edward Coke, *The First Part of the Institutes of the Laws of England* [1610] (London: More, 1629).

barbarism, culture lanced against the occult, and antiquity against novelty. The quest is *de diversis regulis juris antiqui*, for the depth and plurality of ancient *regulae*, meaning norms of practice, rules for life (*praecepta vivendi*), the ground of laws that form the living models for the modern tradition.

Take up again the concept of a foundational discourse. The literary dialogues of law depict an architecture and habitation that has to be entered and inhabited. Law is not simply clothes, though it is also vestment and habit, as Gary Watt most elegantly argues, it is perceived as a building, a frame and structure, an ichnography or floor plan for life.[29] Here we may note the old sense of a norm, which is that of an architect's set square, a device for measuring rectangles, for creating building blocks and ensuring right angles. The foundation is a stone, earth compacted over time, and to examine such bases is to listen to the chatter of stones, the dialogue of that which has survived and lived on. This literary portrayal of law, the sciography of entry into the place and discipline presents the seriousness, the *gravitas* of the undertaking in variously depicting the temple (*templum*), tower (*turris*), the castle (*castellum*), the citadel (*arx*), the dwelling (*aedes*) of legality as the benign yet arduous site of the lawyers offices and of the exemplary life that they should lead. This is matterphorics, the generativity of serious things, giving birth to what matters, choosing the intellectual and here juristic friends whose company of ideas we will keep. This is also what the French legal philosopher Pierre Legendre terms the dogmatic function which, in an obscure legal argot, is that of *instituere vitam* – of instituting life through the time-honoured images that the literary tradition of law passes on through its architecture and collections of texts.

The dialogue of foundation provides a hearing for the multiplicities of law's past. It institutes the institution, the habitation and commonality of the specific legal regime and in doing so, in setting these foundation stones it indicates inevitably that there is far more than just law involved. From a humanistic perspective it is evident that the specifically legal quality of texts is an accent, an argot and stylistic flourish within the vernacular language but one which has obviously enough to be approached first as language, as text, and above all as utterance. It is literature, writing in its most general sense and sensibility, inclusive of the architectural, artistic, vestimentary and ceremonial, that inaugurates law in the social, as matter and as presence, tone and

---

29 See Gary Watt, *Dress, Law and Naked Truth* (London: Bloomsbury, 2014).

practice. Beyond the myopia of literalism and the absurdities of *dura lex* or strict law, the disciplines of philology, linguistics, rhetoric and hermeneutics all provide modes of access to the broader scope, more generous purposes and wider arrays of intendment and meaning that place law within the humanistic embrace of the *ars iustitiae*, the art of justice. Law, in other words, without literary skill, imaginative expression and erudite interpretation, is nothing. It exists as writing and without its letters, and in a technical sense, its *belles lettres*, it would simply sleep as an improbable attempt to terrorize the public sphere by means of a dictatorship of reason and a tyranny of rules.

The community of disciplines is necessary to the rigour of law and by similar token the poet lawyer, the humanistic jurist, the legislator and judge conceived as authors and read as literary legal expressions provide the point of our entry, social and individual, into the realm of law as the mainstay and practice of the art of justice. The legal mind, *mens juridica*, is supported by and expressed through an extensive and elaborate training not simply in law but in letters, in the writing and reading of law as well as of interpreting it, of interpreting it justly, and systematizing it elegantly. As Anne Teissier-Ensminger puts it, in conformity with an expansive tradition of such elision of form and content, the Renaissance, the second revolution of the interpreters, imbibed law with a fresh élan and a novel spirit of the expansiveness of the discipline: 'the litterarisation of law is here focused upon answering the key question of legal humanism, which is that of knowing the extent to which the writing of law can, without disfiguring its object, satisfy aesthetic criteria'.[30] The question is best posed as that of justice: can law be done well, which is to say can legal rule be elegant and ethical, expansive in its resources and apposite in its applications.

In a practical sense, the literary quality of law is initially a pedagogic interest and opening. We come to law through literature and through its own literarity. The introduction to law is through its imagery, its narratives, its cases, portrayed both in fiction and other social media, and then again through its own reports and spectacles. The literary is the avenue, the *via regia*, of access to law both in the sense of wanting to study law and become a lawyer, but also in the related sense of what used to be termed *elegantia iuris*, or the eloquence and elegance of legal expression itself. The island of jurists discussed most directly in *The Republic of Jurists*, is precisely a didactic search for

---

30 *Fabuleuse juridicité* at 407.

the institution and office of the lawyer in its apogee. The Republic transpires to be an archipelago inhabited by the greatest jurists, the 'panjurists' who founded, honed and relayed the tradition of Roman law. In the familiar trope of utopia and atopia alike, the eager students sail for this unknown sphere and after being blown off course arrive on unfamiliar shores. Upon descending from the ship, the inauguration of the students into the elegance of jurisprudence is undertaken through encounters with the most literary legal figures of the past, the great reformers, the finest stylists, the poet jurists who have passed the test of excellence that Plato's *Laws* had dictated as being the criterion of acceptance into usage and so long-term survival.

The journey takes place via the poets and Ovid: 'You must employ your time: time glides on with speedy foot, nor is that which follows so good as that which went before.' [31] Thus the journey to the archipelago *Respublica iurisconsultorum* to interrogate the herculean jurists responsible for a law that is *lumina et numina* – both illustrious and ineffable. The protagonists are welcomed in their inquiry, their search being to learn law a second time, for themselves, to make it theirs and thus to become jurist poets capable of wit and invention similar to that displayed in Judge Smith's cryptogram. The great jurists are teachers and their first interlocutor – entry as one says for content – the Roman jurisconsult Minucius, selected because his is the most elegant house on the island, is concerned most directly with independence of thought, defined as intellectual propriety and probity of thought. This leads, somewhat in the manner of Vico's lessons on education, to the methods and criteria best able to effectuate the optimal congress and most fruitful intercourse of 'poetry, eloquence and law'. There are, for Minucius, three desiderata that will temper the harshness of law with the elegance poetry and so foster justice.

The first is percipience, meaning a sense of context and of the political significance of doctrinal issues. Its opposite is the defect of vexatious litigiousness, petty squabbles, heated and personal disputes between rapidly atrabilious practitioners. Frivolous and inconsequential debates distract and divide jurists and the polity over matters of no significance. The second desideratum is elegance of thought: 'is jurisprudence an art invented to tire the spirit? We cannot remove the natural beauty of this science: she is born to regulate public and particular affairs, and

---

31 For ease of reference, I have used Gennaro, *La République des jurisconsultes* (Paris: Nyon, 1768) at 5.

to form the mind in the spirit of justice'.³² To achieve this goal means attending directly to the purposes and intendments of the relevant rules, interpreting them for the benefit of those subject to them in a lucid and ethical manner. Obscurity, cavilling, chop logic, captious distinctions, and needless complexity denigrate and demit the institution. And finally, third point, broadest of all, humanistic civility is pitched against juristic barbarism. There are men, Minucius intones correctively 'who are prickly, sad and cold, without any light in their spirit; they lack eloquence, method and justice'. These authors confuse their own delirious statements for maxims of law, their writings are utterly tedious, they are lazy, ignorant charlatans who contribute nothing to doctrine and simply bore their readers with hapless irrelevancies and pompous and ugly prose. The beauty of jurisprudence is lost on them and so too the art of justice is turned to ashes.

Following Minucius, a tableau of famous jurists follows and their theme, from Alciato to Budé, Aneau to Bodin, and then Badouin, Hotman and others of the Gallic tradition are all variously cited for their contributions to law as also to *bonae artes*, the humanities, to erudition and justice, to good writing and inventive thinking. These are the desiderata of a witty and engaging jurisprudence, the story of how one comes over time to befriend the law and to know justice. Gennaro provides the most explicit defence of the art of law as a liberal and pluralistic literary endeavour, but we find it elsewhere in both common law and civilian accounts of legal studies. Thus Barthélmy Aneau, one of the great Toulousian jurists, author of several works on aesthetics, begins his *Jurisprudentia* with the ritual invocation of the celestial and natural sources of law: 'Divine and legitimate was the first law, by virtue of which Justice was drawn down from the heavens into the world' and provided the inspiration for equitable jurisprudence.³³ Law is inscribed on adamantine rock, while justice is drawn on soft stone, but in each instance it is expressly from the temple of the human mind, and from mortal hearts – *mortalia cordæ virorum* – that all virtue extends.³⁴ There follows a series of vignettes of the great lawgivers and the most renowned of jurists, mythical figures and divinities are mixed with a diversity of historical authors including reference to the *Utopia* of Sir Thomas More and praise of his erudition as a cosmopolitan learning. At its best and most attractive, jurisprudence is true philosophy – *vera*

---

32 *République*, at 10.
33 Barthélmy Aneau, *Jurisprudentia* (Lyon: Saggittaire, 1554) at 5.
34 Aneau *Jurisprudentia*, at 8.

philosophia – and plays a founding role within and as part of the study of the arts.

The common lawyers are to the same effect and indeed Sir John Cowell inaugurates his dictionary of law with the express opinion that 'a lawyer professes true philosophy, and therefore should not be ignorant (if it were possible) of either beasts, fowls or creeping things, nor of the trees from the cedar in Lebanon to the hyssop that springs out of the wall'.[35] That expansiveness and commonality of thought and learning is replicated throughout the early modern tradition, Anglican and continental. Law is a 'science liberal' and it requires careful study of all the disciplines though, as noted, most directly philology, rhetoric and, because dialogue is dialectical, philosophy. To borrow from Sir John Davies, poet, lawyer, one-time Attorney General of England, and contemporary of that great sage and chef of common law, Sir Edward Coke, 'is not the Professor of law a star in the firmament of the Commonwealth? Is not his house an oracle . . . to a country?'[36] The poet, for Tacitus and for Davies, precedes and follows in the wake of the jurist, as their beginning and their end, their origin and their legacy. This is because the lawyer is in office a teacher and host to living well, at their best and most erudite they are guides to rights and dignities, honours and eloquences, fictions and other formulations that will act ethically and appropriately in volatile situations. The discourse of law is a part, as the English Judge and lawyer Sir John Dodderidge put it, of a larger conversation, and legal elegance, not to strain the point, being the ability to speak appositely and so justly in the frequently cacophonous disquiet of tense conversations and heated conflicts.

Returning to the greater theme, the common core of the juristic tradition, and of jurisliterature in its most generous sense, is that of recognition and expatiation of a liberal and poetic practice of legal criticism firmly embedded in the community of disciplines and fully cognizant of the creative character and visceral role of law in the polity. This is because fiction and law lie down together, image and dogma circulate as works of architectural construction and imaginative fabulation. The Republic of Lawyers is a subset of the Polity of Letters, which fact is most evident in the necessity of approaching law through its literature. The poem, the inaugural address, the preparative, the enchiridion, the *Institutes*, both civilian and common law, the various foundational

---

35 Sir John Cowell, *The Interpreter* (London: Roycroft, 1607) fol. 4r.
36 Sir John Davies, *Discourses* (London, 1615) 282.

Commentaries on the laws, are all exercises in Plato's seriously lighthearted, heavy yet witty, exercises in pedagogy of the multiple actors in law. Literature acts as the portal of entry to the juridical, to legislation, judgment, interpretation and commentary, and the principal pedagogic works are best understood not simply as calls to law but as literary *parerga*, prolegomena and in plainer language overtures, preludes, openings into the juristic that provide our initial image, vision and perspective upon legality, its institutions and purposes, its collections and texts, its manifestations and expressions, both plastic and oral. These are what inaugurate our knowledge, form our perceptions and draw us to law. It is the monumental and visible public presences of legal institutions, the popular relays of legitimacy and authority, the theatre of juridical performances, as well as the literatures, fictive and juristic that now engage and entrance as the aura and form of the legal.

The definition of law in the greatest of Western compilations is explicitly framed in terms of art and elegance: the word law (*ius*) derives from that of justice (*iustitia*), to which Ulpian adds: 'For, in terms of Celsus' elegant definition, the law is the art of good and the fair.'[37] It is not enough to be law alone. A jealous, exclusive, obscure and myopic *dura lex* or inflexibly strict law would neither attract nor commend embodiment. There is always something more, an alien will within jurist and legality, and this is defined as legal elegance, the poetic capacity to align rule with equity, and to conform the text to art and justice. The poetic as elegance references the assonance of the text, the appropriateness of its figures, the harmony of decision and the ease of outcome. The poetic as invention and creation through the use of code and rule book infuses law and provides access to the drive of judgment, the innermost recesses of the legal mind. As Cormack notes with his characteristic insight 'it is in this meeting of law and poetry as twin arts for making something in language, for using language to produce an effect in the world, that we can most accurately speak of a poetics of law or a legal poetics'.[38] Yet poetry should not be confused with law. This may seem obvious but critical legal thinkers are fond of citing Percy Bysshe Shelley who intones famously that 'poets are the unacknowledged legislators of the world'. As argued here, poetry as harmony of expression and creativity in decision is a crucial ingredient

---

37 'Est autem a iustitia appellatum: nam, ut eleganter Celsus definit, ius est ars boni et aequi.'
38 Bradin Cormack, 'Paper Justice, Parchment Justice: Shakespeare, Hamlet, and the Life of Legal Documents', in Donald Beecher et al. (eds), *Taking Exception to the Law: Materializing Injustice in Early Modern English Literature* (Toronto: Toronto University Press, 2015) at 47.

of legal elegance and of juristic eloquence. It is pivotal to deciding and captures brilliantly the dimension of choice and the ethics of juridical interpretation. The poet jurist seeks to fit judgment to circumstance and when these align justice is done.

In the strange yet illuminating case of *Jeffrey Stambovsky v Helen Ackley* a New York court had to determine whether it was phantasmal misrepresentation for the seller of a house to fail to disclose that the house was haunted. The facts were that the owner had for some time advertised and conducted poltergeist viewing tours of her home and had reported the spectral apparitions she had seen in national and local press. Her close encounters with spirits was known in the local community and raised the legal conundrum of whether the law should recognize hauntology and hold the seller liable for non-disclosure of a material fact that the buyer could not, with due diligence, have discerned for himself. The Judge, Israel Rubin, acts poetically in a dual sense. First, he has to decide a point *ab novo*, one, that is, which has not come before the courts before and so requires invention of a solution. Secondly, where the spectral and imaginative are concerned the sources should fit the subject matter of dispute. The Judge moves immediately to cite to the Ghost in *Hamlet*: 'Pity me not but lend thy serious hearing to what I shall unfold.'[39]

Contrary to expectation and against a strong dissenting judgment which argued that 'if the doctrine of caveat emptor is to be discarded, it should be for a reason more substantive than a poltergeist', the decision handed down was in favour of the buyer. The reasoning was equitable and elegant: '*Ex facto jus oritur* (law arises out of facts). Where fairness and common sense dictate that an exception should be created, the evolution of the law should not be stifled by rigid application of a legal maxim.' The logic was *bifrons* or bifold. First, having gone out of her way to inform the public that her house was possessed by poltergeists, she was estopped from denying their existence to the vendee. Second, and poetically, the duty to inspect could not be taken to cover the parapsychic, psychogenic or invisible and so did not preclude rescission of the contract. For the same reason, an 'as is' clause in the sale could only cover the physically evident and not apparitions: 'It should be apparent, however, that the most meticulous inspection and the search would not reveal the presence of poltergeists at the premises or unearth the property's ghoulish reputation in the community.' In

---

[39] *Stambovsky v Ackley* 169 A.D. 2 d 254 (1991).

sum, and *eleganter*, the ghost receives a spectral determination, the fair and the equal is achieved though the poetic harmony and intellective discrimination of theme and expression.

The decision in *Stambovsky* is not, and Judge Smith would clearly accede to this, a literary fiction, but it renders a poetic justice, skilfully using William Shakespeare as the source of legal invention. The poltergeist meets a ghost and by this legal fiction the case is seriously heard and the judgment unfolded in an apposite and ethical fashion. That poetry plays a part in law, and in a manner similar to music, in that it harmonizes, narrativizes, provides images and in this case treats an image as an effective form of contractual action, does not mean that poets should be legislators. The beauty of literature is that it opens up the doors of legal perception, it guides, attends, motivates and changes the act in law, but it is not itself a law. The tendency of critical legal scholars, or Brit Crits in particular, has been to view Shelley's poetic declaration of bards as unacknowledged legislators somewhat unpoetically. Poets are not and should not be legislators, nor do they seek recognition as law makers. They are best when resisting law and instituting rather the conditions of freedom, anarchy in thought, intellection ungoverned by rules, conceiving, experimenting, thinking askew. To legislate is to give laws, to reduce justice to legality, whereas for Shelley the opposite is true and poetry undoes law by exceeding it:

> Poets are the hierophants of an unapprehended inspiration; the mirrors of the gigantic shadows which futurity casts upon the present; the words which express what they understand not; the trumpets which sing to battle, and feel not what they inspire; the influence which is moved not, but moves.[40]

The poet seeks an order unconstrained by law, a beauty of thought and expression that exceeds reduction to commandments, a legislation that is not juridical but rather amicable, volitional, anarchic and free.

---

40 Percy Bysshe Shelley, *A Defence of Poetry* (1840).

2 The discipline of law

The judicial recognition of the legal existence of a ghost with which case the last chapter concluded is an instance of poetic justice in the sense of a creative decision with literary connotations and sources. To borrow from Vico again, '[m]en of limited ideas take law for what the words expressly say'.[1] Thus the authority of the Bard played its proper role. The case is also an excellent metaphor for the common law tradition as a timeless, incorporeal, and seamless web. Our Lady Common Law, as she used to be called, exists, according to the sages of the unwritten knowledge as a system of precedents. What is oldest is best, the prior has priority, and, as the continental critics of common law used to like to say, the impulse is to repeat mistakes. The Civil law tradition, however, is no different. Its *univeralia* also reach back to the XII Tables of Roman Law from almost half a millennium before Christ and latterly to the Bible and the Ten Commandments. The Tables – *Duodecim Tabularum* – were inscribed on bronze tablets, in rhyming verse, and were learned by rote and sung by school children in Cicero's time. The Bible has the Commandments inscribed not once but twice on stone and the biblical text itself became both scripture and model for Western legality. Antiquity triumphs over novelty, both in theology and law. While we will encounter changes in this pattern, new technologies and media of legal dissemination in the last chapter, it is still the case that the primary *poiesis* and inscriptions of law are monumental, forming a visible and significant part of what can be termed the written city. Eternity and art, Latin maxims and ornate costumes are still and will likely long remain the apparel and appearance of law in public spaces.

Gold leaf, bronze statues, columns, thresholds, murals, thrones, rotunda, domes and inscriptions are the physical signs of legality that the denizens of city or town will daily encounter. Law's enigmatic presence is highly visible yet also withdrawn and somewhat esoteric. As

---

1 Giambattista Vico, *The New Science* [1744] (Ithaca: Cornell University Press, 1984) at 93. (cix).

the *Psalms* have it, *in imagine ambulat homo*, we walk as images and amongst images and each in their turn inhabit a context and open and close to the eyes. As to context, history and place, the court is most usually close to the Church. In New York the court buildings, from the Surrogates Court to the Supreme Court are grouped next to City Hall, on Centre Street. At the heart of the complex is the Roman Catholic Church of St Andrews, predating the courthouses, and with the inscription *Beati qui ambulant in lege Domini*, meaning blessed are they who walk in the law of the Lord. Angels hold an escutcheon (shield) aloft, and further Latin invocations of the Messiah and statues of Saints adorn the façade and its columns. Thresholds, columns and a certain giganticism mark the surrounding courts, where the inscribed motto on the facia of the Supreme Court building states, all caps, 'the true administration of justice is the firmest pillar of good government' and stares down on Foley Square. Those that enter the front of the Criminal Court do so through an arch bearing the roman numerals MDCXXV, and are confronted immediately with rotunda murals of Justinian and Blackstone. In London, because the child seldom falls far from the mother, the Old Bailey, the Central Criminal Court, is proximate to St Paul's Cathedral, and the inscription inside the modern version of the building states, again all caps, 'Moses gave unto the people the laws of God'. At the top of the building's 67-foot high dome, made famous in part by the movie *V for Vendetta*, stands a gold leaf statue of Lady Justice. At the entrance, the angels of truth and fortitude stand guard and signal transition to another time and space, or in Kafka's diction, a coming 'before the law' where, ironically, much of what takes places happens *in camera* or privately under vaulted arches, in chambers, in an emptied court.[2]

The law, belonging visibly to the monumental city, its architecture a throwback to imperial visions, its columns, pedestals, statuary, murals, portraiture and costumes all generate a sense of the opulence and separation of the juridical from the quotidian. One steps into another world, a heterotopic space and atmosphere of antique tradition, ancient hierarchies, old ways of doing things. The *poiesis* of power thus manifests in multiple ways to position the viewer, the auditor, the reader in a preordained hierarchy, as a subject of the *dispositif* or apparatus of lawful disposition of social places. The distribution of law's sensibilities is

---

2 For an entertaining and insightful account from the inside of the Old Bailey, see Andreas Philippopoulos-Mihalopoulos, 'To have to do with the law', in the eponymously edited collection *Routledge Handbook of Law and Theory* (London: Routledge, 2019) at 475.

complex and begins architecturally with the design of different points of entry, different interior spaces, corridors, chambers and forms of spaces for seating, for judges, lawyers, jurors, litigants, press and laity. These all have their own significance and meanings as modalities of control of role, of what and who is seen, of angles of vision and degrees of importance or visibility and audibility accorded to specific actors. The High Court of Bombay, for example, a Victorian colonial gargantua, has a separate entrance for judges, above which local craftsmen carved a monkey in robes, holding a sword in one hand and the scales of justice in the other. The simian face has a blindfold that covers only one eye, the other peers out over the entering judiciary. Over the lawyers' entrance there is a fox wearing a collar and a barrister's band. Both are intriguing resistances on the part of the sculptor to the overtly imperial and evidently imposing design of the building. While the cautionary monkey is seen only by judges, the separate entrances and pathways within the courthouse spell out a clear and distinctive hierarchy and variable levels of access to spaces within the building.[3] This forms a key part of what Mulcahy and Rowden in their recent study of court architecture term the geopolitics of courthouse design which focuses attention upon the spatial and material dimensions of law's social presence, taking account both of the exterior, the façade of buildings but also attending to the interior dynamics of circulation, waiting, holding and performing.[4] Cells, corridors, docks, boxes, bars, benches, thrones, screens all play their part in manifesting the various hierophantic, guild, clerical, disciplinary, observational, carceral and abject routines that the players – the *dramatis personae iuris* – will enact.

There are two further dimensions of the built environment of law, the enclosure of justice in the city that deserve attention. The first is that of an inherited and in our case Christian battle with death. For the self-titled 'most holy' Roman Emperor Justinian, the temple of justice and the text of the *Corpus iuris civilis*, which was for him the codification of all law, were alike the markers of eternity, the permanent and

---

3 See Rahela Khorakiwala, *From the Colonial to the Contemporary: Images, Iconography, Memories, and Performances of Law in India's High Courts* (London: Hart, 2019) at 136–43. See also, on power and court spaces, Linda Mulcahy, *Legal Architecture: Justice, Due Process and the Place of Law* (London: Routledge, 2011).

4 Linda Mulcahy and Emma Rowden, *The Democratic Courthouse: A Modern History of Design, Due Process and Dignity* (London: Routledge, 2019). There is also Judith Resnik and Denis Curtis, *Representing Justice: Invention, Controversy and Rights in City-States and Democratic Courtrooms* (New Haven: Yale University Press, 2011).

unchanging house of truth. These texts were not to be interpreted but simply to be applied as the immutable expression of divine and human knowledge, in that specific order. The buildings that house the law reflect, in inscription, often in Latin, in architecture and flow of personnel, in their lists and 'do not enter' signs, not only an enclosed order but a perdurance and longevity that also belittles and outlives the mortal coils that temporarily ambulate through their confines. A building is precisely what lives on, what does not die as humans die and these stones, the granite, marble, brick, wood and plaster renderings all signal a permanence beyond mortality. The very matter of buildings signifies an atropaic gesture towards death, a glimpse of the beyond or, in the words of Christ: 'in my Father's house are many mansions: If it were not so, I would have told you. I go to prepare a place for you'. The theological fiction of an afterlife is repeated in legal imagination in the divine authorization of the law courts and its other deities, internal and exterior. The English legal sage Sir Edward Coke, whose personal emblem was of the sun shining down on an empty throne with the motto *alter solus*, the other sun, remarks at one point, in that self-same spirit, that 'earth is the suburbs of heaven'.[5] Equally to the point, the stones chatter according to their distinct temporality and long distance tones. That we cannot hear what the stones say does not mean that the walls are silent. They too speak beyond their mere inscriptions.

The second and correlative point is what, borrowing again, because she is generous, from Gandorfer, I will term matterphorical.[6] This is most directly to say that while law seeks to portray a system of rules that are general in nature and abstract in their orderings, this self-image omits a key aspect of so-called black letter law, as also of jurisliterature, which is that even its letters are material, coloured, haptic, housed and bound or now more often flickering across a screen but nonetheless spatially organized, material and mattering. The argument against abstraction, the matterphorical critique of laws of theory that deny the onto-epistemological relevance of the housing and carriage of ideas, as

---

5 Coke, *First Part of the Institutes*, fol 4a. The Biblical quotation is from the King James Version, John 14:2.
6 Daniela Gandorfer, *Matterphorics: On the Laws of Theory* (Duke University Press, forthcoming) at 31 remarking of matterphorical thought, [that it] is less a rhetorical device than a practice of and commitment to opposing transcendent thought, detached analysis, representationalism, and Cartesian rationalism. As I will show later, matterphorical thinking takes (and gives) place in theories of immanence, and is, if taken seriously, less prone to colonizing modes of thought. It differentiates based not on entities and their categorizations, but by means of material-discursive practices that precede human and non-human entities.

if the materiality of the bodies, locations, and media of their transmission were incidental, immaterial, are a significant obstacle to approaching the literary practice of law as a space-time of performances whose context and transitions are material to their meaning. The very word for law derives from *nome* and thence *nomos* – from which we derive normative or rule bound – means earth, dirt, the *humus* in the human. Matter precedes law. The lines on the thoroughfare, the traffic lights, the registration plates, the signposts, indeed the fingerposts, the guards at the doors of the law, the barcode that provides entry to the law library all signal in material-discursive fashions, as writing, the grammatology of the built environment that ensures that law circulates with the bodies of its circulators.

Matter, of course, and the materiality of buildings, which too will fall in time to ruin or replacement, contradicts the message of a sempiternal legality, the adamantine rule of a tellurian nomos, in the very moment of enacting and announcing it *sotto voce* through the walls, statues, paving stones, serried steps, columns, and inscriptions. Even Sir Edward Coke, at one point, in a discussion of courts and officers of the weald, remarks 'and thus have we wandered in the wilderness of the laws of the forest . . . wherein (as the studious reader may well perceive) we have respected matter more than method'. The error Coke makes is implicitly to separate matter and method, to bifurcate and so, potentially at least, to oppose matter to method whereas matter, as the foregoing discussion proposes, is the foundation of method, and method is the melody, the rhythm and tune that attention can discern in the material world or most just earth. For present purposes, however, the key point is that of the priority of matter, our durance in the built environment, and what it signifies in visible material terms prior to thought and before the enactment of any record, rule or law. The old phrase was 'nude matter' according to the law dictionaries or 'matter in deed' as distinct from matter of record, but that is simply to affirm again that materiality precedes classification and normative iterations, however age old they may claim to be. It is for this reason that law claims to be a building, to have the permanence of stone, to be built, like the Church upon rock.

I noted in the previous chapter the tendency of jurisliterature to title introductory works of law buildings (*aedes legum*), towers (*turris iustitiae*), and to intimate that these were panjuridical characteristics, features of the temple of justice and the uncut cloth of law. The narrative is one housed in the matterphor of architecture as archetype of legality and signifier of the anachronic and abstract essence of the juridical in nature and the divinity. The early common lawyers were much absorbed by such a theme of juristic recognition of custom and use so ancient as to return to nature herself and thence if not to God, at least to great proximity to the divine. Law has its reasons of which reason knows not.[7] These are related in part to the intrinsic precedence of the English and of Albion, and in part to a history that disappears into the native soil. The Druids, we learn rather charmingly, were the first law givers and did not use writing but rather oral transmission, 'nude matter', to convey their traditions and usages.[8] Other genealogies referenced a law that returns to Brutus, the first King of England, or to other giants, to Samothes the God of knowledge and to Ceres, the patron of Anglia and amongst the first inhabitants of this Island. The literary tradition of English law, in other words, has a divine inspiration and within the Christian tradition, according to the redoubtable one time Chancellor, Sir John Fortescue, common law – but recall that for his era and beyond, 'God is English' – was the most excellent of all, sublime and 'superior to the civil law in that [we] accord more closely to the scriptures and the writings of the Church Fathers'.[9] Elsewhere, in the leading early modern treatise on the history of the English tradition, *Origines juridiciales*, we are told with no uncertainty that English laws are 'founded upon the law of God, and extend themselves to the original Laws of Nature, and the universal Law of Nature, and were not originally *Leges Scriptae* . . .' presumably because they predate writing or in the Greek tradition are written on the heart and inscribed in practice not in the dead letters of books.[10]

The common law is a specific variant of the Western legal tradition that stems from Rome. The *mos britannicus iuris docendi* or English tradition of teaching law has its own peculiar jurisliterary form that aligns it to mythologies of antiquity and closeness to divinity that are distinctively local in exposition but differ from continental variants only in the refusal of history by virtue of England's break with Rome and consequent hostility to continental legal traditions. The *Corpus iuris civilis* and the works of the glossators remained a principal source

---

7 Most memorably, Sir John Fortescue, *De Laudibus legum Angliae* [c. 1460], trans. Lockwood, *On the Laws and Governance of England* (Cambridge: Cambridge University Press, 1997).
8 Selden, *Jani Anglorum facies altera* (London: Bassett, 1610); Spelman, *Of the Four Law Terms: A Discourse* (London: Gillyflower, 1684 edn).
9 Fortescue, *De Laudibus*, at 4–5.
10 William Dugdale, *Origines juridiciales or Historical Memorials of English Laws, Courts of Justice, Forms of Tryall* [1666] (London: Savoy, 1671) at 3b.

of early common law, which after all remained recorded primarily in Latin until the eighteenth century, but any direct reference was viewed as succumbing to 'the tincture of Normanism' and the sophistic casuistry of the Roman Church. Thus alternative literary sources and poetic forms were needed that would fill the gap left by the excision of the primary text of Western law. For the common lawyers, for English law, the myths of divinities, Druids, and of sources 'beyond the memory of man', 'time out of mind', or since 'time immemorial', standing in for the vanishing point, the image of beginning inscribed in earth and air. The lack of a foundational text or pandect required a site of disappearance, the figures of Hobbes' decaying sense that evaporate into an image, a maxim, a dogma. *Non Angli sed angeli* – not Angles but Angels was the pun that Pope Gregory propagated on the English, and that the common lawyers later turned to their own use.

The foundational narrative has to be one of necessity and as nothing human is of itself a necessity, authority and justification of the legal system lie in a mythic recourse to the law of nature as divine writ evidenced by the nomos of earth, here meaning the patterns and usages that persist and become the fictive figures of people and nation. The *lex terrae*, the law of this earth, the particular island, as it is historically termed is the ground of the imagined community and the immanent mode of its governance. Ancient custom and antique law are inscribed in the soil, carrying with them an aura of divinity: 'positive laws are framed in the light of natural law and reason and from thence come all the grounds and maxims of the common law, for that which we call common law is not a word new, or strange or barbarous . . . but the right term for all other laws'.[11] The soil, brute ground remembers what the Holy Men of law admitted, though as a virtue rather than a defect, was never written: 'which Text was never originally written, but has ever been preserved in the memory of men, though no man's memory can reach the original thereof'.[12] The skin of the earth is the mnemonic of legality which those learned in law carry within them as ambulant earthlings and interpreters of the fruits of tellurian reason accessible, in the last instance, to juridical divination but not to common sense.

The key point in the narrative of laws' *habitus*, its buildings, spaces, architecture, and earth is that law finally vanishes into the oracular, what psychoanalysis defines as the void, the beyond of tradition and

---

11 Henry Finch, *Law, or a Discourse Thereof in Four Books* (London, 1627) Bk 1 at 74–5.
12 John Davies, *Le Primer Reports des cases and matters en ley* (Dublin: Franckton, 1615) at fol 2b.

faith. The latter term, fond to lawyers in its latinate modes of *de fide*, *fiducia* and fidelity, is defined by the Anglican William Perkins as 'belief in what is not', and this characterizes well both the exigency of commitment and the disappearance of reason. Law is too old, too prior, too holy to question.[13] The tradition is carried esoterically – druidically – by its priests and their pronouncements will also have a vanishing point which is usually framed in the recourse to Latin maxims or dogmatic formulae. Thus the maxims of law, printed originally in red typeface, mimicking Book 50 of the *Digest, De Verborum significatione*, are the cenotes of doctrine, sinkholes for the disappearance of law. Much has been written on juristic maxims as grounds of law and the import is primarily that they are the point of no return, the last bastion, beyond which lies only nothingness, pure void, mere faith. Thus for one of the early modern commentators upon Fortescue, to take just one example, the maxim is so named because it is the greatest – *quia maximus est* – and from this exorbitance emanate all the inferior rules of law. The maxims themselves, however, are expressly mysteries and must remain so because they cannot be questioned but only apprehended and obeyed: they are 'not to be dived into, but adored, because of their coparceny with Divinity'.[14]

The house of the law, in other words, and borrowing from our earlier case, is haunted. An invisible superior being and their edicts resonate in the stones, move with the visible tracks, the fingerposts of the land, and beat as the rhythm of the heart. The Inns of Court in London which originally housed the legal profession and is still home to a significant portion of the Bar, was expressly understood to be modelled upon the nine orders of angels: 'Here I might compare your state (but that you are men) unto the heavenly Ierarches, for that you have the three things that Ierarches have, that is, Order, cunning

---

13 William Perkins, *A Discourse of Conscience. Wherein is set downe the nature, properties, and differences thereof: as also the way to get and keepe good Conscience* [1608] (The Hague: De Graaf, 1966) at 6: '*faith*, is a perswasion whereby we believe things that are not . . .' The lawyer Edward Whitehouse, Fortescutus illustratus, *or a Commentary on That Nervous Treatise* 'De laudibus legum angliae' (London, 1663), at 126 equally offers 'faith is the evidence of things not seen (and in) seeing him that is invisible' we also see his precepts and commands – *praeceptum et mandatum*.
14 Edward Whitehouse, Fortescutus illustratus, *or a Commentary on That Nervous Treatise* 'De laudibus legum angliae' (London, 1663), at 122. Sir John Dodderidge, *The English Lawyer: Describing a Method for the Management of the Laws of this Land* (London: More, 1621 edn) expands the maxim to text: 'Matters de Record import in eux (per presumption del ley, pur leur hautnesse) credit'—matters of record are of themselves (by presumption of law, on account of their antiquity) to be believed.

and working . . .' Perkins concludes that every hierarchy follows the conformity and likeness of God.[15] Again, at the risk of stating the obvious, the stones, statues, courtyards and elaborately intricate skein of chambers signify a juridical ordering of space, a labyrinthine hierarchy and embellishment of the aura of the profession. The chatter of stones, the badinage of bricks, conveys the *arcana imperii*, the mysteries of rule, in a trans-historical and esoteric fashion. The law is there to lend an ear, to provide a hearing, to listen to the complaints of plaintiffs and, as work on the architecture of the Inns has shown, the aggregation of the houses of law in central London, viewed from above, form an ear.[16] The audition is the mode of justice and for common lawyers forms an auditory and auricular tradition, an oral inheritance resident in an angelological guild and in the acoustics and symbolic emanations of buildings that dictate the various participants' spatial positioning and place in the hierarchy of ineffable orders.

It is in both the cladding and the corridors, the folkways and argot of the profession that the unwritten source and higher law, which the texts and writings of the early sages record as *mos britannicus*, the Anglican way of doing things, the common law of England, resides. It is in technical terms, ironically in the circumstances, an unwritten law – *ius non scriptum* – which means that it is not a codified system, neither Roman nor Norman nor continental at all, despite the Latin. The monumental character of the unwritten law signals something more than writing, access to that which the written denotes, the invisible choir and source of legal authority as such. What that means for the jurisliterary tradition is that things that are not, invisible entities, ghosts and other images, spectres and further inventions can emerge more easily, can gain dogmatic status, doctrinal recognition, become part of the embrace that is the populist virtue and expansiveness of common law. That the history is of a textual tradition that is unwritten simply, or not so simply, means that the narratives are recorded incidentally, unsystematically, ad hoc and frequently somewhat haphazardly. The precedents are now taken down verbatim and judgments published, usually after review by their author, but the cases in their numerous appearances are just that, cases, one after another and in

---

15 Gerard Legh, *The Accedens of Armory* (London: Totell, 1576) at fol. 135v.
16 See David Evans, 'The Inns of Court: Speculations on the Body of the Law' (1993) 1 *Arch-Text* 17, and for elaboration of the auditory theme, see Goodrich, 'Auriculation', in Christian Delage, Peter Goodrich and Marco Wan (eds), *Law and New Media: West of Everything* (Edinburgh: Edinburgh University Press, 2019).

no particular order and according to no acknowledged schema. They form the books of interpretation whose sources and authorizations are primarily themselves and failing that, the divinity, the Bible, the red letters of a maxim, a Latin phrase or two.

Take what in legal terms is a reasonably recent example, a case from the first quarter of the eighteenth century, The King *against* The Chancellor, Masters and Scholars of the University of Cambridge.[17] The strange facts of the case, reported as it happens by one Strange, were that the Reverend Richard Bentley, fellow of Trinity College, Cambridge, was suspended from his position, and all titles and rights of fellowship were removed – *ab omni gradu suscepto* – by order of the congregation, a university Court. The facts were as follows and fellows. One Conyers Middleton, Doctor of Divinity, had appeared before an earlier Vice Chancellor's Court complaining that Bentley owed him a certain sum of money. A process was issued to Edward Clark, the beadle, to compel Bentley to appear at the next congregation sitting. When the beadle – an officer of the University – served the process upon Bentley, the latter, 'upon discourse between them concerning the process . . . contemptuously said the process was illegal and unstatutable and that he would not obey it . . . the Vice Chancellor was not his judge', and *stultè egit*, he had acted foolishly. At the next hearing of the Congregation, the Court removed Bentley's degrees, for contempt of the Vice Chancellor's Court. The Congregation reasoned that 'time out of mind' there had been a court held before the chancellor or vice chancellor and that 'time out of mind' such Court had removed degrees for 'contumacy or reasonable cause'.[18] It was against this decision that Bentley appealed.

Two questions were mooted upon appeal. The first was that of whether Reverend Bentley was in contempt of court for saying that the Vice Chancellor '*stultè egit*' or acted foolishly. The second and more serious issue was that the Congregation had never summoned Bentley to their hearing and had not provided any other notice of the time and place of their sitting. He had therefore been unable to defend himself. The lack of notice was insuperable and Justice Fortescue proceeds to state that:

> The laws of God and man both give the party an opportunity to make his defence . . . I remember to have heard it observed by a very learned man . . .

---

17 *R v University of Cambridge* (1823) I Strange 557.
18 Ibid., 557–8.

that even God himself did not pass sentence upon Adam, before he was called upon to make his defence. Adam (says God) where art thou? Hast thou not eaten of the tree, whereof I commanded thee that thou shouldst not eat? And the same question was put to Eve also.[19]

The language of the judgment may seem archaic but the offence of contempt of court still exists and is not infrequently exercised at common law. Interestingly, and in consonance with the decision in *R v Cambridge University* contempt that occurs out of the court, 'scandalizing the court', is in most jurisdictions not an offence and so not subject to penalty. The rule that the defendant must be heard is also vigorously upheld. What is significant about the decision from the perspective of the *mos britannicus* and the jurisliterature of common law is the style and the sources for the determination, one unwritten, and one scriptural.

Of the unwritten image of time out of mind, invoked a Biblical three times, the logical corollary of such non-residence in the *caput legum*, the legal cerebellum, is inhabitation elsewhere. First, in the ancient University of Cambridge, a 'corporation by prescription', but a definite site and series of buildings, of offices where merely mortal members momentarily reside. Second, 'time out of mind there has been a court', which again is an architectural space, be it a hall, a stage, a forum, a corridor, a chamber, an alcove, or a garden. All are geopolitical locations, spatial sites, modes of congregating and controlling an audience through the built environment or less often arboreal arrangements. The latter possibility is raised by the third recital of time out of mind as being 'the custom for the chancellor or vice chancellor to summon a congregation' of those that George Ruggles in his *Ignoramus* nominates the fog bound wits of Cambridge.[20] Here it is custom inhabiting the seat and offices of chancellors, use over time, patterns of behaviour inscribed in the very molecular structures of the institution. These talismanic words are the figures of law, the ley lines, as Professor Haldar has recently and imaginatively represented, of the culture and *mores* of common law.[21] Consider, as the report reaches its conclusion, that the Chief Justice regales the audience with the

---

19 Ibid., 567.
20 George Ruggles, *Ignoramus or the English Lawyer* (London: Gilbertson, 1662).
21 Piyel Haldar, 'Ley Lines: The Imaginary Origins of Common Law', in Goodrich and Zartaloudis (eds), *The Cabinet of Imaginary Laws* (London: Routledge, 2021): an essay that 're-imagines another history of common law as one that emerges from the deep layers of the earth.'

pronouncement that '[i]t is the glory and happiness of our excellent constitution' that someone who believes themselves wronged by a court decision can appeal the case, as the Reverend Bentley has here done, much aggrieved by loss of his tenure and degrees. Glory, the angelic force of an imaginary constitution and its operation *in excelsis* via the ministrations of the Chief Justice reinforce the sensibility of a natural force and higher law invisible to those who do not have the power to see what is not there.

Even more intriguing in terms of the law of the land and the stones upon which it is writ, is the shift, the metonymic transfer from the *lex terrae* to the Garden of Eden and the story of original sin. One verdant legal space invokes another. The weight of authority, the *auctoritates deorum et poetarum* are overwhelming. Bear in mind that in the parable from Genesis all of the parties to the illicit gustation are punished and also that none of those found guilty admits responsibility, and it is the serpent, who is not given the benefit of *audite et alterem partem*, the right to be heard, that is sanctioned the most severely. There are even in the Garden of Eden persons and non-persons. The other signal feature of the passage from which the Chief Judge cites is that in this original trial the Judge is God and fears that the humans may become gods as well: 'And the Lord God said, Behold, the man is become as one of us, to know good and evil: and now, lest he put forth his hand, and take also of the tree of life, and eat, and live forever', he is expelled from the garden, 'to till the ground from whence he was taken'. There could be no more signal expression of the hierarchy of *nomos* and the penalties for crossing its lines of division between the distinct orders of governance than the invocation of expulsion from Eden for tasting of the forbidden fruit at the instigation of the serpent and vicariously of Eve. So Adam claimed, and the Biblical order of things, the separation of human and divine but not of law's 'knowledge of things divine and human', was ordained and instituted.[22]

---

22 One could equally utilize examples from the US, as, for example, *Church of the Holy Trinity v United States* 143 U.S. 457 (1892) in which the Supreme Court observed in a very direct fashion that America is a legally authorized Christian nation:

> If we pass beyond these matters to a view of American life, as expressed by its laws, its business, its customs, and its society, we find everywhere a clear recognition of the same truth. Among other matters, note the following: the form of oath universally prevailing, concluding with an appeal to the Almighty; the custom of opening sessions of all deliberative bodies and most conventions with prayer; the prefatory words of all wills, 'In the name of God, amen'; the laws respecting the observance of the Sabbath, with the general cessation of all secular business, and the closing of courts, legislatures, and other similar public assemblies on that day; the churches

The garden, the tellurian law and justice of the earth again appears in a more recent instance of higher sources. In the Court of Appeal, in 1995, in a case concerned with local authority powers to act for the purposes of 'benefit, improvement or development' of Council owned land, Sir Thomas Bingham MR opines that the issue is biblical: 'To the famous question asked by the owner of the vineyard: "Is it not lawful for me to do what I will with mine own?" (St Matthew xx. 15) the modern answer would be clear: "Yes, subject to such regulatory and other constraints as the law imposes."'[23] As the issue concerned judicial review of local authority action – the banning of deer hunting on council land – the Judge continued in biblical tones to state that for the local authority the answer was 'no, it is not lawful for you to do anything save what the law expressly or impliedly authorises. You enjoy no unfettered discretions. There are legal limits to every power you have'. The trial Judge Laws had determined that the Council had prohibited deer hunting simply on the basis of 'distaste or ethical objection' and concluded that '[t]here is no trace of a considered judgment as to the effect which the ban would have on the management of the herd, or how the deer were to be conserved in the light of it'.[24] Sir Thomas, however, took a contrary view on the latter point, suggesting that in his interpretation the 'beneficial of . . . their area' was entirely permissive: 'The draftsman would have been pressed to find broader or less specific language.' Paradoxically, this would appear to provide little by way of fetter or limit to their power or, put differently, the land could stipulate its own benefits, a tellurian justice that could not be challenged, a governance by the earth as represented through the Council. In biblical argot, do what thou wilt, would seem to be the Appellate conclusion. The law gives and the law taketh away.

Other Gods, this same earth in different parts, gains distinct recognition in other jurisdictions. Take another example, a recent decision

---

and church organizations which abound in every city, town, and hamlet; the multitude of charitable organizations existing everywhere under Christian auspices; the gigantic missionary associations, with general support, and aiming to establish Christian missions in every quarter of the globe. These, and many other matters which might be noticed, add a volume of unofficial declarations to the mass of organic utterances that this is a Christian nation. In the face of all these, shall it be believed that a Congress of the United States intended to make it a misdemeanor for a church of this country to contract for the services of a Christian minister residing in another nation?

23 *R v Somerset County Council ex parte Frewings* [1995] 3 All ER 20.
24 *R v Somerset County Council ex parte Frewings* [1995] 1 All ER 513.

of the Indian Supreme Court.²⁵ The case revolved around a vexing question, one of increasing ecological as well as theological topicality: can the earth bring a law suit, can dirt, *humus*, be recognized as a legal person? The occasion for the dispute was a claim by the Hindu community that in 1528 the Muslim Emperor Babur had invaded and built a mosque over the site of the Hindu deity Lord Ram's birthplace. According to previous case law, affirmed by the English Privy Council, a deity was a legal person and could bring an action in law through their human representatives, the *shebaits* or alternatively custodians of the religious community, if there was a deity present and worshipped in visible forms in a specified place. The condition for such legal personality was vivification meaning a vivified image of the deity to which manifest presence – be it a painting, a statue, or some other emblem of higher being – offerings, ceremonies and supplications were made. 'It is sufficient to state that the deity is . . . conceived as a living being and is treated in the same way as the master of the house would be treated by his humble servant.'²⁶ The requirement of a vivified image – termed an Idol – ordains that the deity have a tellurian presence but under the prior case law it is the manifestation of the deity that triggers juristic recognition and the status of a legal entity capable of bringing an action. In the case of Lord Ram there was only the testimony of the earth and the claim that close to half a millennium ago the site had been home to reliquaries and ceremonies that celebrated the birthplace of the deity.

In one case, an exception of sorts, with a pataphysical ring to it, an empty space, air and atmosphere, a hole, was treated as a deity. In *Sri Sabhanayagar Temple, Chidambaram v State of Tamil Nadu*, the issue before the Court was that of the mismanagement of a Hindu Temple and the juristic difficulty of treating the site of worship of Lord Siva, the Supreme Being, as a legal entity.²⁷ Dedicated to the Supreme Being the Temple had no idol and thus, in the Supreme Court's later determination, failed the most basic test of legal personality which is that of manifestation: 'The Supreme Being has no physical presence for it is understood to be omnipresent – the very ground of being itself . . . [and] For the reason that it is omnipresent it would be impossible to distinguish where one legal entity ends and the next begins.' Thus the requirement for an idol to give form to a shapeless being and

---

25 *Siddiq v Suresh* (November 2019) Supreme Court of India (Civil Appeal Nos 10866-10867 of 2010).
26 *Siddiq* at para. 140.
27 *Sri Sabhanayagar Temple, Chidambaram v State of Tamil Nadu* W.As.182 &183/09 (2009).

this, where Siva was worshiped most usually through the figure of a 'Lingam', a symbol. What was difficult in the *Chidambaram* case was thus the form of manifestation because the Temple: 'contains an altar which has no idol. In fact, no Lingam exists but a Curtain is hung before a wall, when people go to worship, the curtain is withdrawn to see the "Lingam". But the ardent devotee will feel the divine[ly] wonder that Lord Siva is formless i.e., space which is known as "Akasa Lingam"'.[28] The decision was thus that the empty site, a blank wall was a representation of the secret of divinity and the being of nothing was idol enough if curtain and altar could limit a space which thereby somehow framed the deity as manifest in the particularity of their absence.

An empty space, a hole, is defined in Daumal's phantasmology as 'an absence surrounded by presence . . . an absence of someone and not of something'. He proceeds to explain that 'it is the pierced substance that determines the shape of the hole and not the absence which that presence surrounds . . .'.[29] Here the court recognized what Mark Fisher terms 'the agency of the virtual . . . that which acts without (physically) existing'.[30] A haunted space nonetheless still requires the actuality of surrounding substance – the house that is haunted, the not yet of future being, the spectre that awaits a tellurian event for its manifestation to realize in the house or on the altar. There is obviously a difference between a past being that haunts and a future presence that spectrally awaits but the analysis of the presence of the formless allows the later decision in *Siddiq* to recognize patterns unearthed in the ground as past signs of ceremonial investment of the dirt with divine presence. There were illicitly installed idols, introduced in 1949, but the material evidence was geological and antique. What better evidence of tellurian presence could there be than the earth itself? If it could be shown through archaeological and stratigraphical evidence that Lord Ram was worshipped at the site, as claimed, then the earth in effect became the idol of the deity or at the very least gained legal personality by association with the deity. The reasoning of the majority allows for the fact that changing beliefs and altered circumstances require the creation of new juristic entities to reflect the development of the creed.

---

28 *Chidambaram*, at para. 3.
29 Daumal, 'The Pataphysics of Ghosts', in *Pataphysical Essays*, at 91.
30 Mark Fisher, *Ghosts of My Life: Writings on Depression, Hauntology and Lost Futures* (London: Zero Books, 2014) at 18.

The spectre of the earth as manifesting the presence of a deity, an aura and atmosphere that connects to a place which gains juridical personality by virtue of that relationship, provides the closest that one could come to a representation of *lex terrae* or the law of the earth. Custom and use over time become law. All that is needed is faith, what the Romans termed *de fide instrumentorum*, belief in the marks, patterns, tracks of usage as manifestations of the nomos of the earth, the voice of the soil. The examples of law as ordained, established, part of the fabric of things and inherent in the biblically generated structure of the social can be multiplied indefinitely. The architecture and architectonic of the legal order are expressions of an establishment that drifts out of sight, out of mind, out of time into the umbrageous dominions of angelology and celestial beings. Entire domains of common law emerge from biblical analogies and, as in the last example of governmental overreach, decisions predicated upon the general concept of the rule of law as a restraint upon the exercise of power, slip easily back into biblical vineyards, the fecundity of the earth and ultimately to the Garden of Eden. From Lord Coke, to Lord Atkin to Lord Bingham an aura of the ineffable, a sense of something more, the brute extancy of the establishment, the eternity of the bricks and stones, of durance and endurance, strikes at the heart of those that come before the law. Here is a point that cannot be moved beyond, because this is the final word – *non plus ultra* – the façade and visage of how things are and, in some less definite yet equally imposing sense, how they have always been. This, in its way, is legal right, meaning law before right, established law, granted that right is simply at root *recht,* and hence at base a tautology, the duplication of establishment, the right of right, the law of law.

Does the chatter of stones still matter? Do the well-hewn building blocks of the courthouse, the bevelled steel, the domes, the columns that cry out to the heavens, the steps that ascend to the portals, yet tell a story and convey the residence of power as the prior ordination of things, what is and ought to be? If one looks, and here is the peroration on these parliaments of principle, at the roots of doctrine and judgment, the valence of time-honoured, biblical origins and their justifications, the gravity of the spirit and the flesh of its incarnation are readily visible and thoroughly audible. The monumental city shouts out its Latin inscription, beside the Court, on the arches and rotunda, the murals and skylights. *Beati qui ambulant in lege domini*, blessed are they who walk in the laws of the Lord sings from a Church next to the New York Supreme Court and Court of Appeals. The legislative assembly in Karnataka, India, has 'Government work is God's work'.

The praise for good government on the portals of other court buildings is but an 'o' away from God's government. Atop the dome of the Old Bailey in London is the Goddess Justitia. A divine augur. A gold symbol. Then inside the building, under an elaborate Old Testament mural, are the words, all caps, 'MOSES GAVE UNTO THE PEOPLE THE LAWS OF GOD'. From the often invoked commandment that thou shalt not kill, to the parable of the rich man for whom it was harder to enter the kingdom of heaven than for a camel to pass through the eye of a needle, the references, allusions and innuendos of Christian values are both frequent and deep rooted. The bulk of the English law of tort, and specifically the development of the neighbour principle, as is well known, arises from an analogy to Christ's second commandment in the Gospel of St Matthew, '[t]hou shalt love thy neighbour as thyself', and is one of Lord Atkin's many recourses to theological sources.[31] References to the parable of the good Samaritan abound in tort law and elsewhere, the forum of conscience being a short hand for the dictates of a Christian moral law.[32] Equity is the domain, after all, of discretion, of acting in good conscience and rectifying merciless general laws where the determination leads to injustice. A welter of amorphous concepts that allow a bending of the ruler, a Lesbian measure, to fit the uniqueness of the case.

Divination, intuition, the semiotics of the earth in the form of custom and patterns of usage allow for judgment that mimics that of Solomon and takes up the higher cause. The judges may no longer be self-styled as *sacerdotes*, holy men, or cenobites, as they were historically, but the self-perception of the role of judge has many similar features to this day, in one instance requiring the decorum of ceremony and the solemnity of robes to qualify as law, rather than 'mere administration'.[33] The rules for contempt of court remain in place and it is still a criminal offence, subject to summary imprisonment, to ignore, disrespect, or disrupt a judge in session. Coke's suburbs of heaven, inhabited by

---

31 *Donoghue v Stevenson* [1932] AC 562.
32 The good Samaritan plays a role, for example in *McLoughlin v O'Brian* [1981] QB 99: 'It is partly at least because a wrongdoer ought to expect that good Samaritans will rush to the rescue of the injured that he is legally liable for injury which they may suffer in the course of rescue.' In the US case of *Mills v Wyman* 3 Pick. 207 (1825) where 'the plaintiff acted the part of the good Samaritan, giving him shelter and comfort until he died'. In *Berkson v GOGO LLC* 97 F.Supp.3d 359 (2015) where the legal rights of the Good Samaritan are intriguingly discussed. In *Barnes v Yahoo* 570 F.3d 1096 (2009) provision 230 (c) (1) of the Communications Decency Act, titled 'Protection for 'good Samaritan' blocking and screening of offensive material' gains discussion.
33 *MacPherson v MacPherson* [1935] All ER 105.

the glory, happiness and excellence of our unwritten constitution and its inchoate rights, provide the ground or more accurately the clouds from which emanate the language of determination. The sanctity of contracts, the requirement of good faith, the estopping of falsehood, are phrased and founded upon the holy order of things. *Falsus in uno, falsus in omnibus*, false in one, false in all, as the maxim goes.[34] Religion and law, according to the Renaissance lawyer Fulbeck, do lie down together.[35] The point made here is that from such copulation its issue are born.

---

[34] *Indymac Bank v Diana Yano-Horoski* 890 N.Y.S. 2d 717 (2009), reversed on other grounds in 2010.

[35] William Fulbeck, *Direction, or Preparative to the Study of Law; wherein is shewed what things ought to be observed and used of them that are addicted to the study of law, and what, on the contrary part, ought to be eschewed and avoided* [1599] (Aldershot: Wildwood House, 1987), I have slightly altered the quotation for my own purposes. The citation is found at 3: 'for religion, justice and law do stand together....'

3 Allegories

The value of law lies in its use, in what rhetoricians term the *actio*, performance. Signs, as the previous chapter has essayed to elaborate, need their material support, the striation of the earth, the marking of a border, the inscription of a building, the printed text, the armorial flag or, most physically active of all, the speaker's elocution. For rhetoricians, it is delivery that is the quintessence of the art and this is a matter of carriage, timbre, gesture, indigitation, as well as atmosphere, built environment, vicinity and architectural channelling of place and position. Speech is physical, described even by the lawyer Plowden as an exercise in the vibration of the air with the tongue.[1] The *poiesis* of law, the inventiveness of its abstractions and the flight of its figures to abstract generality should not preclude or otherwise hide the soundly material bases of its various signs, images and words inscribed, as already tabulated, in the physical structures and corporeal manifestations that constitute the offices and institutions of the juridical as mobile entities, and tralatitious moments in and of the polity.

Advancing now to the rhetoric of law, to the jurisliterary genre in all its diversity and cross-cultural divagations, the *antiquae fabulae* play their part and it is necessary to recognize, prior to any linguistic analysis or textual criticism that materiality plays a foundational role, it matters greatly, in the verbal performance of law. All of the oaths that lawyers take, and make others take, involve ceremonial acts and objects, a rite that shapes and places the body of the juror, the Judge, the Bishop, the Crown, the witness, the accused as the case may be. It is important to recollect that, as discussed in the previous chapter, this goes back to early law, to the indistinction of 'knowledge of things divine and human' which both Roman and Common law use as their definition of

---

[1] Edmund Plowden, *The Commentaries or Reports* (London: S. Brooke, 1816) at 82: 'For words which are no other than the Verberation of the Air, do not constitute the Statute, but are only the Image of it, and the Life of the Statute rests in the Minds of the Expositors of the Words, that is, the Makers of the Statutes.'

jurisprudence.[2] In one telling of the story of the Ten Commandments, Moses inscribes the laws on the Tablets of stone and carries them back to the tribe. On seeing the Idol, his anger was so great he was about to smash them when he saw that the writing had vanished from the stone and he became aware of their terrible weight. Deprived of the celestial text the blank Tablets revert to the heaviness of rock and crash to the earth. The allegory of law broken, vanished then broken again exemplifies well the metaphoricity of meaning as being in significant part also a facet of occasion and event, context and performance. One viewing of the scene of delivery of the law is precisely that it ceases to exist once its material support has been lost. The disappearing text that reverts to its celestial source no longer exists for us because lacking material form it cannot be a mode of custom and use and in the absence of some element of inscription, be it in the earth, pathways, social habits, political practices, the body, the heart even, there is no vivified image, no incarnadine temporal expression that records and makes such law available. In short, with the breaking of the Tablets of stone, nothing was instituted, neither site nor place of legality could emerge until this foundation stone was actually placed and the juridical inaugurated as a legitimate building block upon which the house of law could subsequently stand.

An institution houses a literature, a normative genre of discourse which emanates in specified forms from specific sites, the archives, libraries and now databases. Isidore of Seville defined institutional writings as propaedeutic texts which taught precepts for living and the rules of faith – *praecepta vivendi et credenda regulam*.[3] The institution is a theological and latterly juridical enterprise of social cohesion and since the early drama of the Ten Commandments has required both housing and investiture for entry. The function of the legal institution is that of instituting persons, legal entities that can act in law, be it corporations, priests, deities, ghosts, earth, space, holes, parsons or persons. These are the *dispositifs*, the institutional forms of registration and disposition of social actors and action. The two faces of law that Isidore aligns with ecclesiastical texts, the *regimen animarum* or

---

2 Sir John Dodderidge, *The English Lawyer: Describing a Method for the Management of the Laws of this Land* (London: More, 1621 edn) at 28–9: 'Secondly, they say that the knowledge of the Law is affirmed to be *rerum divinarum humanarumque Scientia*, it doth containe the knowledge of all divine and humane things.' On the image of the Ten Commandments, see Carolin Behrmann, in 'On *actio*: The Silence of Law and the Eloquence of Images' (forthcoming).
3 Isidore of Seville, *Etymologies* (Cambridge: Cambridge University Press, 2008 edn) at VI.ii.50.

cure of souls, and the sword of divine vengeance, are inherited by secular law in the mode of instituting life and rule, *oikonomia* and the spectacle of the political, in Agamben's terms.[4] The institution of life, emergent from the buildings is the result of ceremonial initiation and investiture procedures whereby officials are ordained and persons are entered into offices. The requirements, amongst others, historically include 'proficiency in letters' and rites of opening of mouths, kneeling, presentations of papers and other passports to entry. The letters of the law arrive always already marked matterphorically and metaphorically. Long before the envelope is cut, the book is opened or the icon clicked the stage has been set and meaning emerges indelibly marked by the institutional *dispositif* of law from which it emanates. This multimodality is intrinsic to any narrative comprehension of the discursive practices of judges and jurists.

The dominant figure of legality, according to the barrister and poet George Puttenham is that of allegory or extended metaphor. As has often been commented, this is the figure of governance and according to the faux Latin maxim: *Qui nescit dissimulare nescit regnare* – one who does not know how to dissimulate does not know how to rule. To dissimulate is to speak metaphorically '*allegoria* is when we do speak in sense translative and wrested from its own signification, nevertheless applied to another not altogether contrary, but having much conveniency . . .'.[5] *Allegoresis* can reference falsehood but its more expansive meaning is simply that of the inventive and active mode of thinking. Transferring sense, stretching concepts, inventing connections, rendering narrative vivid, enacting images in language are the modes of mobilizing thought and moving an audience.

Allegory, for Puttenham, is thus what might be thought of as *veritas falsa*, both true and false, meaning inventive, imaginative speech or writing seeking to generate both conviction and persuasion: 'To be short, every speech wrested from his own natural signification to another not altogether so natural is a kind of dissimulation, because the words bear contrary countenance to their intent.' That said, all speech is in some degree imaginative and of 'contrary countenance' simply because it comes from another and, more profoundly, because rhetoric teaches that the natural meaning of words is not something

---

4 Giorgio Agamben, *The Kingdom and the Glory: For a Theological Genealogy of Economy and Government* (Palo Alto: Stanford University Press, 2011).

5 George Puttenham, *The Art of Poesy* [1589] (Ithaca: Cornell University Press, 2007) at 271.

that is ever certain: literalism, as Vico remarked, is for those of limited ideas, ignorant of semantics and of tabid inventiveness. As he proceeds to propound, following Aristotle, judgment is always probable and certainty is simply another word for particularization or individuation.[6] The momentum of ideas and the unfolding of dialogue are always plural and expansively polysemic endeavours.

The figures – the fabrications – of legal discourse do not differ from those of other literary genres and so, prolegomena aside, context, atmosphere, and corporeality acknowledged as mattering, it is time to turn to the practice of legal *poiesis*, the inventions of juridical discourse and the aesthetic of its expression. The rhetoric of law, its style and simple figures have been much analysed, distributed, classified and ordered. To advance upon that requires a slight change of focus at the level of legal discourse. The literary practice of legality is here understood as an inquiry into the mobility and inventiveness of juristic practice. This is a matter of metaphor as the figure of transfer and change of meaning, the sign of the development, the unfolding novelty of legal texts and juridical opinions as each new instance and authorial expression devises its own advance upon what came before. *Allegoresis*, the extended and extensive effect of metaphoricity then becomes the figure of the literarisation of legal discourse. Rhetoric challenges law, and the excavation and analysis of its literarity is threatening to the supposedly logical order and complacency of its positive expression. The advenience – the advent, calling out or interpellation – of jurisliterature constitutes a minor jurisprudence in the sense of the minor developed by Deleuze and Guattari and taken up by Panu Minkkinen in relation to law.[7]

A minor jurisprudence is a deterritorialized and distinctive subcultural language within, and contestatory of a major argot or discursive formation.[8] In this sense, jurisliterature is an attempt to insert the literary into the legal, to open a space of becoming, the *mundus imaginabilis*, the dominion of sensibility inside the major and often desultory realm

---

6 Giambattista Vico, *New Science* [1744] (Ithaca: Cornell University Press, 1984) at 93.
7 Gilles Deleuze and Félix Guattari, 'What is a Minor Literature?' (Robert Brinkley trans) (1983) 11(3) *Mississippi Review* 13, 16; see also Gilles Deleuze and Félix Guattari, *Kafka: Towards a Minor Literature* (Minneapolis: University of Minnesota Press, 1986) [Dana Polan trans: *Kafka: pour une literature mineure*] (first published 1975). Panu Minkkinen, 'The Radiance of Justice: On the Minor Jurisprudence of Franz Kafka' (1994) 3 *Social & Legal Studies* 349.
8 On the subcultural character of minor jurisprudence, and its critical role, see James Gilchrist Stewart, 'Panic at the Law School! An Argument for Legal Subcultures' (forthcoming).

of juridical prose.[9] The initial step in minoritizing is thus to acknowledge and expand the analysis of the figurative character of juristic expression, to focus upon the symptoms of the literary, the slips and flights of expression, the figures of affect that slip past the author and provide the sense and drive of the text. To admit to the minor, to 'the radiance of justice', to the strangeness of language not only revives the radical humanist tradition within Western law, but also potentially, in being pushed further, creates a novel genre of writing law outside the confines of literalism and in a polylingual and allegorical modality. It is as a minor jurisprudence that jurisliterature has and will continue to challenge the complacency and the claim to dominance and control that the major jurisprudence, the analytic, positivistic, literalist and frequently boring enterprise of legal closure likes to claim. A minor jurisprudence is an excluded language seeking to surface in and reorient the dominant tradition. It is one that claims to change the meaning of the rulebook while asserting the potential for transition that lurks in veiled form or is hidden in the major language. The children – Freud's sons – take on the parents – Freud's father – but in a political rather than an oedipal sense. Everything is political in this accounting, meaning that the linguistic subversion of law is an assertion of difference, a right to a minor language internal to the idiom of governance, a drive to generate a novel space and more embracive collectivity of utterance within law.[10] The minor thus propels the other, the narratives, fictions, languages of literary invention, the challenges of plurality of meaning, into the argot of an exclusory and idiomatically opaque legality. As Minkkinen propounds it, minor jurisprudence both exposes the fiction of the major tradition and opens the door, as artistic and authorial inscription, as storytelling, to a politics of desire and initiation of a political programme of self-creation, of acts of interior law giving through the creative art of writing.[11] Similarly for Teissier-Ensminger, it is the function of jurisliterature to wrest law away from the exclusive control of sclerotic traditions of repetition and the pickle jar of precedent.

---

9 I discuss this in terms of the history of minor jurisdictions in Goodrich, *Law in the Courts of Love: Literature and Other Minor Jurisprudences* (London: Routledge, 1995). For more recent discussion of the minor as unconstrained, and of *minumenta*, see Goodrich, 'How Strange the Change from Major to Minor' (2017) 21 *Law Text Culture* 30.

10 Deleuze and Guattari, 'Minor Literature?' 18: 'There is no subject: there are only collective arrangements of utterance – and literature expresses these arrangements, not as they are given on the outside, but only as diabolic powers to come or revolutionary forces to be constructed.'

11 Minkkinen, 'Radiance' at 357.

The *topos* of jurisliterature is primarily pedagogic in the humanist and cultural sense of providing access to and modes of entry into law. The aesthetic of the juridical is the most visible and socially available manifestation of the institution and administrative presence of governance. The literary, figurative and imagistic are the modes of alluring and seducing the subject and the neophyte, the minor meaning here the young, into the narrative and phantasy of law as allegorically portrayed. Legal elegance (*elegantior iuris*), the delectation of the text, *amoenitas* meaning the charm or fascination of legality is the most frequently used term, are the juristic modes of disseminating and transmitting the juridical form of life while equally opening the law to entry, inculcation, renewal or contestation. Jurisliterature is the mode of teaching law to the public, to youth, to neophytes and belongs, as Teissier-Ensminger so brilliantly captures, to the arts that instruct and institute life – *artes vitam instruant* – as opposed to merely ornamenting existence.[12] To instruct is to invest, induct and institute a form of life according to juristic *mores*, to inculcate offices, actors and actions as intrinsic to the form of life of the polity. It is the collective ethos of law that is composed and conveyed aesthetically in the mode of jurisliterature or, to borrow again from the inexhaustible Teissier-Ensminger, '[t]he civilization of the image and the evolution of pedagogy have in effect combined their effects so as to encourage jurists, in a single movement, to teach through laughing (*ridendo*) and painting (*pigendo docere*), which is to say, to use humourous imagery', to introduce new generations to the specialized guild of lawyers.[13] What is at issue is instituting law and life, *instituere vitam et legem* and the task of the jurisliterary is to open up the space of such invention and effect and tell the narrative of its unfolding over time and persons.

The minor is visible in minor forms and as regards the jurisliterary this is a question of entering juristic texts through the allusions, figures, and the *allegoresis* of the disquisition, be it legislative, precedential, administrative or propaedeutic. A slight and simple instance can be taken from an anxious yet seemingly ordinary case as a mode of entry to an analysis. In *Levine v Blumenthal* the question raised was that of whether a purported accord and satisfaction between the defendant lessee, a manufacturer of 'women's wearing apparel', and the plaintiff landlord, was enforceable. In 1931 the defendants had signed an

---

12 Anne Teissier-Ensminger, *Fabuleuse juridicité: Sur la littérarisation des genres juridiques* (Paris: Garnier, 2015) at 237.
13 Ibid., at 823.

indenture, a two-year lease at a specified, incrementally increasing rent. The depression put the manufacturer in a parlous financial position and they told the landlord that 'they could not pay the increase called for in the lease because of adverse business conditions'.[14] The landlord claimed that for the second year he had accepted the lesser rent on account, or until business improved. When the tenants vacated a month before the end of the lease, he sued for the unpaid month and for the arrears owing for the previous 11 months.

Justice Heher is faced with one of the most perplexing of doctrinal issues in the common law of contract. If parties vary an agreement that both have entered into for financial gain, does there need to be additional consideration or emolument for the alteration of terms? This is a vexed and controversial issue both then and now. Civilian jurisdictions have no such requirement and common law has oscillated in its view: for some courts doing the same thing in different circumstances is sufficient proof or consideration for the variation, while for others, performing an existing legal duty cannot be *quid pro quo* for a new promise but is rather presumed to be extortion. Justice Heher is comprehensively in favour of the latter view: 'It is a principle, almost universally accepted, that an act or forebearance required by a legal duty owing to the promisor that is neither doubtful nor the subject of honest and reasonable dispute is not a sufficient consideration.'[15] The allusion, of course, is to the opening sentence of Jane Austen's *Pride and Prejudice*: 'It is a truth universally acknowledged, that a single man in possession of a good fortune, must be in want of a wife'. A minor and elliptical reference that plays in all likelihood to a preconscious sense of the reader, but it is precisely in this glancing quality and the incidental character of the perlocutionary act that the power of the usage resides.

Three features of the allusion, this anaphoric novelistic reference and oblique litterarisation of style, require analysis. I will term these respectively covering, persuasion and enforcement. The primary point is that the fictive borrowing is covert and partial, a seemingly incidental feature of a reasoned opinion that moves on to discussion of doctrinal issues in a commensurably bombastic manner. Everyone, even white male (although by curiosity of nomination transgender) judges cover, as Kenji Yoshino has laudably elaborated. Covering here

---

14 *William Levine v Anne Blumenthal* 186 A. 457.
15 Ibid., at 458.

means initially that disfavoured traits are hidden.[16] In this case the litterarisation of the judgment is obscured by the failure to cite the source and by the alteration of the wording, allowing a covert insertion of the topic into the decision. What the Judge wishes to effectuate by this technique is a disavowal of the subjectivity of decision-making and the uncertainty of the law. Justice Heher covers both the inventiveness of the determination and the affective application of literary sources to judicial practices of judgment. The Austenian ellipsis hides the anxiety of decision, the controversy as to the law, and the difference of approach amongst adjoining jurisdictions, behind the claim to the (almost) universality of the principle of consideration.

There is a duality, a layered quality to covering insofar as it is the creative character of the reasoning, the reliance upon what Derrida terms the incalculable, which is here taken to mean the corporeal, subjective and performative aspects of doing and deciding, and simultaneously a marginalization and in this case effective denial of the literary referent.[17] Taking the latter feature first, the marginal is frequently the most indicative facet of paintings, texts, and here I would argue judgments. According to the art historian Morelli, who greatly influenced Freud, in determining the authenticity of an artwork, the clearest signs of forgery were in those peripheral facets of the painting, as for example the fingernails, distant background, ears, where the forger has paid much less attention to details. These are crucial clues as to authorship and in Freud's terminology are slips that convey the unconscious drive of the speaker.[18] The literary reference is covered because it is a disfavoured trait, an expression, however unwitting of affect, but also as a conflicted sign of invention and of authorship which in the fictive domain of legal theory is not the role of the judge but that of the legislator. The judicial role is purportedly more of relay than of invention and so where, as here, the case is liminal, and the rules ambiguous or conflicting, the more necessary the covering of affect and of the subjectivity of judgment behind the claim and corn rows of an impassive and impartial reason.

---

16 Kenji Yoshino, *Covering: The Hidden Assault on Our Civil Rights* (New York: Random House, 2006) at 24.

17 Jacques Derrida, 'Force of Law: On the Mystical Foundation of Authority' in Drucilla Cornell, Michel Rosenfeld, and David Carlson (eds), *Deconstruction and the Possibility of Justice* (London: Routledge, 1992).

18 Carlo Ginsberg, 'Clues: Roots of an Evidential Paradigm', in Ginsberg, *Myths, Emblems, Clues* (Baltimore: John Hopkins University Press, 2013).

Covering is a mode of veiling the drivers of decision and so the further layering of this insertion portends an inexplicit, in Freudian terms, an unconscious narrative. Looking to the context of Heher's recourse to Austen and the universal desire for the security of a marital relationship, it is rapidly apparent that the omnipresence claimed is at best polemical and at worst inaccurate. Consideration, the element of *quid pro quo* that makes the bargain enforceable as an act in law, is as necessary for the variation of an extant agreement as for the original contract which is already supported by exchange of a benefit and detriment. The Judge protests volubly and repetitively that there can be no disputing the doctrinal requirement: 'It is elementary that the subsequent agreement, to impose the obligation of a contract, must rest upon a new and independent consideration.' Heher continues to expostulate that '[t]he rule was laid down in very early times', and then again asserts that '[t]he principle is firmly imbedded in our jurisprudence that a promise to do what the promisor is already legally bound to do is an unreal consideration'. It is again 'a basic principle' and 'a doctrine that has always been fundamental'. There is recourse, finally, the last refuge of covering, to Latin, that almost universal language, for the principle that the defendant tenant is attempting to assert *nudum pactum* – a bare agreement – as a contract.[19] And then, after these multiple assertions of a glittering and unchallengeable rule *sub specie aeternitatis*, it is contradicted by admission that several jurisdictions do not require any new consideration for variation of an agreement to the benefit of both parties and entered so as to make the transaction work. It is admitted that others of authority have argued that the application of the principle to the variation of terms in an ongoing relationship, is 'mediæval and wholly artificial'. It is acknowledged lastly that 'any consideration for the new undertaking, however insignificant, satisfies this rule'. Thus, payment of the lesser amount on a different day, addition of a horse, a hawk, a robe, a peppercorn, or in our case a promise not to file for bankruptcy would all satisfy the requirement while adding nothing of actual value to the exchange.

The anxiety of judgment is neither uncommon nor lodged in the 1930s depression, although some of the finest examples come from that era of grand style of judgment. Justice Cardozo, in an even more extreme case involving a charitable bequest, manages the following magnificent indirection and circumlocution: 'The longing for posthumous remembrance is an emotion not so weak as to justify us in saying that its

---

19 *Levine v Blumenthal*, 458.

gratification is a negligible good.'[20] In a more recent US example, a company that made use of an offer of free hazardous waste, AggRite, as substrate for pavement construction sued the supplier of the free material for breach of contract. The Judge, Joan Orie Melvin, begins her analysis with the resounding statement that '[i]t is axiomatic that consideration is an essential element of an enforceable contract'.[21] She proceeds to the conclusion that even though the AggRite was given free of charge, and without any discussion, bargaining or dickering of any sort, both parties received a benefit and so there was a contract implied in fact. One could continue to cases where nothing is sufficient consideration, if nothing is genuinely desired. As for example a worthless piece of paper in the view of some of the judges in *Haigh v Brooks*, as more recently expanded in *Browning v Johnson*.[22] The giving of consent becomes the immaterial substance of consideration, or in the language of another English court, the obviation of a disbenefit, a double negative can be consideration.[23] Examples of hyperbole and of contradictory logics could be multiplied but our focus is less on the doctrine than on the rhetorical transfers that occur.

Returning to the example of Judge Heher, the reference to Austen makes subtly yet elegantly evident a process of *allegoresis* that would otherwise likely be hidden behind the language of consideration, the argot of bargain, the expression of apodictic principles and self-evident universalities. The anaphoric reference is to the desirability of marriage and the paradoxical virtue of commitment. Women in Austen's time might sell themselves through marriage to wealthy men, and so too, by parlous logic, the sale of women's apparel should likewise carry its charge and meet its dues. What is significant is that it is women's apparel that triggers Heher's recollection and insertion of Austen, as if to indicate that the principle of marriage settlement, the sum that the spouse agrees to give herself up to, were the source in social conscience and *mores* of the Judge's clinging to the theoretical wreckage of consideration. Marriage was a commercial contract, spousals *de futuro* an executory exchange, and so too in a commodification of both logic and relationship, Justice Heher demands that proper form, convention, the

20 *Allegheny College v National Chautauqua Bank* 246 N.Y. 173 (1927).
21 *Pennsy Supply Inc. v American Ash Recycling Corp.* 895 A.2d 595 (2006).
22 *Haigh v Brooks* 10 A.D. & E., 113 Eng. Rep. 119, 124; and more to the point here, *Brooks v Haigh* 10 A.D. & E. 322, 113 Eng. Rep. 124, 128. *Browning v Johnson* 430 P.2d 591 (1967).
23 *Williams v Roffey* [1991] 1 QB 1, though now doubted, doubtless momentarily, in *MWB Business Exchange Centres v Rock Advertising* [2018] 4 All ER 21.

litany of mistaken precedents, be followed, lest the dam burst. Thus feminine nubility and women's apparel, spousals and rent, He and Her, law and literature, are placed in unreliable yet rhetorically effective juxtaposition. That said, marriage is the exemplary contract and so it is a not uncommon figure in the judicial rhetoric of contractual engagement, agreement, consummation and gains its most celebrated expression in the case of *Hochster v De la Tour* where the court made an explicit analysis of the law of contract as an instance of what was then the contract of spousals *de futuro*, which was then an enforceable contract of engagement:

> As an example, a man and woman engaged to marry are affianced to one another during the period between the time of the engagement and the celebration of the marriage. In this very case, of traveller and courier, from the day of the hiring till the day when the employment was to begin, they were engaged to each other; and it seems to be a breach of an implied contract if either of them renounces the engagement.[24]

The imported allegory has clear and evident purport in asserting, under cover of anaphoric allusion, the narrative of contract as being a question also of Christian good faith, of honouring one's commitment, of the unbreakable bond of the sacred covenant of marital estate which is modelled upon the marriage of Christ to the Church. None of this, of course, is directly stated, but the implication of universality and the structure of the sentence manifest a judicial desire to enforce the original promise made by the tenant to the landlord as a commitment and compact between two parties that was equivalent to the marital vow. Only death or here the end of the lease term would relieve the parties of their duty under the contract, once consummated. It is this narrative of marriage, of perfect union, such as should not be torn asunder, that is invoked as being the custom and use 'laid down from very early times', which is 'elementary', 'fundamental', 'firmly imbedded' and, not to stretch it too far, also in the couple embedded.

The reference to Austen brings with it the *allegoresis* of contract as marriage, the theology of covenant and faith, of immemorial commitments from time beyond memory, of early and repeated custom and use, as also of the ties that bind. There is a heavy weight to the signifier of spousals and Justice Heher draws on this to lend gravamen and colour to his precarious assertions. He also wants, perhaps not so inno-

---

24 *Albert Hochster v Edgar Frederick De La Tour* (1853) 2 L. B. & L. 679; 118 Eng. Rep. 922.

cently, to force William Levine and Anne Blumenthal to stay together, the male landlord requiring the female tenant to stick to her bond, to stay true to her promise, to be a faithful spouse. Justice Heher, to risk a certain nominalism, uses the priority of his name to impose He upon her. Gender plays its traditional role and Anne's word is not to be believed, it is not her bond, and despite the admitted permissibility of parol (oral) modifications of leases her consent lacks sufficient weight. There is both pride and prejudice in Heher's judgment in the precise sense that his reference invokes the disparity of the sexes and a canon law of marriage that subordinates the woman to the man, wife to husband because for most of their history, both civilian and common law have followed the maxim that women are inferior to men.[25] This, in sum, is how it ought to be. A point which can transition discussion to the second feature of *allegoresis*, namely that it is a tool of persuasion. Heher is aware that his position, far from being almost universal is somewhat the opposite. Many jurisdictions allow consensual variation without consideration; civilian legal systems have no requirement of consideration; doctrines of estoppel that were operative in the US from the 1890s also allowed for enforcement without bargain; and even in the 1930s, long before the Vienna Convention on International Sale of Goods, such contracts would frequently be subject to foreign choice of law. Heher is aware that invention is necessary and resorts to the implied literary argument and allegorical figure of promises deserving to be kept as part of the order of things, as virtuous, by nature and divinity ordained as a good, and like a marriage.

The Judge is seeking the support of cultural norms and religious practices to imply a greater weight and legitimacy – a term itself that derives from the propriety of marriage – and the literary narrative that is inserted is the figure that most obviously bears the weight of such *allegoresis*. It is a subtle circumlocution and as adumbrated a mode of covering where in other circumstances a court might resort to a more explicit invocation of equity or justice. Where the decision is less contestable, as for example in a case of undue influence, then the call to the morality, rightness and goodness of the decision can be only indirectly

---

[25] The relevant maxims can be found in the *Digest*: D. 1.9.1 (Ulpian), 'greater dignity inheres in the male sex', and in D. 1.5.9. (Papinian), 'there are many points in our law in which the condition of females is inferior to that of males (*detior est condicio feminarum quam masculorum*)'. William Blackstone takes up the same point on the part of common lawyers. For discussion see Peter Goodrich, Oedipus lex: *Psychoanalysis, History, Law* (Berkeley: University of California Press, 1995) at ch. 5; and more recently *Schreber's Law: Jurisprudence and Judgment in Transition* (Edinburgh: Edinburgh University Press, 2019).

literary in the sense of citation. Thus, a favourite example for its vivid facts, a 51-year-old widow, who had sought spring in her life and in her step, sued Arthur Murray dance school for having extorted payment for 2,302 hours of dance instruction by endless cajolery, flattery, artifice and trickery, when in fact she was tone deaf and could never improve. The terpsichorean muse must ever remain a stranger to her. Judge Pierce, in robustly circumlocutory fashion, concludes that 'in the case *sub judice*, from the allegations of the unanswered complaint, we cannot say that enough of the accompanying ingredients, as mentioned in the foregoing authorities, were not present which otherwise would have barred the equitable arm of the Court to her'.[26] In a word, it is the right thing to do, yet equity too is invoked through indirection and figurative divagation so as to obscure the affect and invention of judgment. The case is represented in ceremonial Latin mode as *sub judice*, the arm of the law is outstretched, the *corpus iuris* is literally to hand, generic authorities are incited, the *auctoritates poetarum* are circulated. The manifestation of equity is purportedly particular and yet is here imposed in the most abstract of manners so as to incorporate again a lengthy history, the dialogue of *Doctor and Student*, the figure of justice, images of sovereign *misericordia*, the sense and sensibility, in short, of doing what is right by virtue of necessary causes, even if juristically speaking they have not been specified in any precise doctrinal detail.

The allegory of *aequitas*, dressed up in a plethora of juristic precedents and cultural values, swarms to support the outcome in conclusory fashion. The judgment needs to persuade other judges, the appellate judiciary in particular – there is nothing worse than being reversed on appeal – and also the tribe of academic commentators, textbook writers, and a wider public when, as here, the topic of conflict is potentially of general interest. A further and much more publicized example can be taken from a more liminal and novel decision in relation to menacing messages sent via Twitter. In *Director of Public Prosecutions v Chambers* at least four genres of literature interact and at times conflict: tweets, statutory edicts, judicial deliberations and drama in the form of a citation from Shakespeare. It forms a fertile ground for analysis, a species of test case for jurisliterary theory, akin to Derrida's

---

26 *Audrey Vokes v Arthur Murray Inc* 212 So. 2d 906 (1968). This is one of many cases against the Dance School's aggressive sales tactics. For a conspectus, see Debora Threedy, 'Dancing Around Gender: Lessons From Arthur Murray on Gender and Contracts' (2010) 45 *Wake Forest Law Rev.* 749.

position in the force of law, but more specific, that entry into another language, crossing the line of the legal prose for the allegorical force of literature is the only mode in which justice – poethical decisions, juris-literary texts – can be created. The calculable encounters the incalculable, the matterphorical, the requirement of a transfer of meaning, the advenience of *allegoresis* as the fiction of law as usual.

The issue prosecuted, appealed and then appealed again was a novel mode of utterance on a new platform, Twitter. Using the microblogging, 140-character limit, platform, the twitter handle @PaulJChambers, the appellant, living in the North of England, had been due to fly to Belfast on January 15 to meet a tweep friend, whose handle was @Crazycolours. A week before he was due to fly, Doncaster Robin Hood Airport was closed due to snow and an exchange relating to the closure ensued:

> @Crazycolours: I was thinking that if it does then I had decided to resort to terrorism:
> @Crazycolours: That's the plan! I am sure the pilots will be expecting me to demand a more exotic location than NI.
> @PaulJChambers: 'Crap! Robin Hood Airport is closed. You've got a week and a bit to get your shit together otherwise I am blowing the airport sky high!!

After some deliberation, the Crown Prosecution Service decided to charge Paul Chambers under sections 127(1)(a) and (3), for so it is writ, of the 2003 Communications Act, with 'sending by a public electronic communication network a message of a menacing character'.[27] Chambers was convicted in the Magistrates' Court and fined a total of £985. He lost his job as a consequence. The conviction was appealed but upheld by Judge Jacqueline Davies of Doncaster Crown Court. She castigated Chambers as an 'unimpressive witness' and his evidence as 'self-serving', concluding that the tweet was 'menacing in its content and obviously so. It could not be more clear. Any ordinary person reading this would see it in that way and be alarmed'. Chambers, in other words, 'in the present climate of terrorist threats, especially at airports, could not be unaware of the possible consequences'.[28] He was ordered to pay a further £2,000.

---

27 *Chambers v Director of Public Prosecutions* [2013] 1 All ER at 150.
28 *The Guardian*, Thursday, 11 Nov. 2010 (Paul Wainwright).

The decision resulted in major media and Twitter protests, with the comedian Stephen Fry offering to pay the fine and the costs of appeal, and numerous journalists pouring scorn on the Judge's failure to comprehend Twitter, tweets and tweeps, while also lacking any appreciation of the parodic character of the posting. The agelastic determination managed the extraordinary feat of turning a joke into a crime. It was this crowd-sourced, cloud-based protest that produced a final appeal to the High Court where, before the appropriately named Judge Judge, the conviction was finally overturned on the grounds that no one responding to the message, neither airport security nor the South Yorkshire Police, nor the lame 630 tweep followers of hashtag @PaulJChambers had in fact been unduly disturbed by the 108 characters of the posting. When it comes before Judge Judge to be judged, the suit has something of the character of a test case on use of the new medium, the meaning of the short message, the context and sociolinguistic impact of the tweet which, after all, was sent a week before the planned travel to visit the avatar or handle @Crazycolours.

A new medium dictates a novel discourse, a different language, a distinct decision, and here most obviously a transgression of the gravitas of law. It poses a threat most immediately in being outside and other to the language of law, an extimacy that seemingly escapes juristic comprehension, a fact that is sometimes noted by the judiciary, although not in this instance.[29] The use of Twitter by #PaulJChambers and @Crazycolours is transgressive in the event both as a form and as a message that includes reference to terrorism, hijacking, and exothermic fulminations. It is in a double sense external to law, transgressive of medial boundaries as also of the limits of legal language, infracting perhaps the ludic prohibition in Roman law of jokes and of plays (*artem ludicram*) in public forums.[30] More than that, a third transgressive feature lies in the reversal of the discursive hierarchy in which the serious social speech of law is handed down a one way street from the Judge to the Court, author to auditor, in the traditional form of juridical edicts and promulgations. Here, however, the public and media outcry, the pandemonium on Twitter,

---

29 In *HM Attorney General v Kasim Davey and Joseph Beard* [2013] EWHC 2317, for instance, the President of the Queen's Bench states: 'Indeed, you may have heard about the juror who went on Twitter or is it Facebook – I am afraid I am on neither – I may be discussed there, but I am not on either. . . .'

30 The ban on jokes is most notoriously to be found in Alan Watson (ed.), *Digest of Justinian* [CE 530–533] (Philadelphia: University of Pennsylvania Press, 1985), at 1985), at liii–liv making jokes a crime (*iniuria est ludos exercere*) and also, at xliv (*De Conceptione digestorum*) forbidding commentaries and interpretations of the written law.

the microblogged maelstrom of critiques of the conviction in the Magistrates' Court and then the Crown Court drove the case to the High Court and clearly influenced the decision, not least because 'ordinary people' were manifestly more threatened by the judges' incomprehension of new media than they were by the tweets under interdiction. What is transgressive is not the diffraction of discourses, the incomprehension manifested between old and new media, forensic text and social media, but rather that the extra-legal in this instance came to play a dominant yet unacknowledged role in the decision.[31]

Context transgresses the literality of law, indeed, to coin a phrase, it 'cons the text', it tricks legality and dethrones legalism. Judge Judge – I can't resist – makes a dismissive reference to the syntactic inadequacy or simple semantic paucity of Twitter, remarking of the tweet in question that '[t]he language and punctuation are inconsistent with the writer intending it to be or to be taken as a serious warning'.[32] It would appear to have been discursively inadequate, grammatically deficient, as a threat. To say that terrorism is ineffective when syntactically incorrect is almost absurd unless one interprets the Judge symptomatically as deflecting from the key transgression which is that in the absence of law, in the incalculable moment of judgment, in the 'High' Court, polysemy intended, it is precisely the extra-juridical, the everyday of social media and internet relay, the strange world of post-law that takes the reins and decides the case. The Judge cannot say that this is a matter for popular decision, for an informal vote, for democratic populism, but that is the context that necessarily drives the particularity of the determination.

There is ample and commendable literature on the input of audio visual links, of internet communication, of pixelated protagonists impacting courts and trials but these are generally functional technical aids to legal control, versions of a virtual panopticon, whereas the case of Twitter is the inverse, a domain that is out of legal control, that recursively and sometimes violently turns on the law and redraws its boundaries in the sciographic mode of a shadow redrawing the sensible form that it supposedly reflects.[33] That form is the law, but it

---

31 For an excellent analysis of this reversal of trajectory, see Helen Carr and Dave Cowan, 'What's the Use of a Hashtag? A Case Study' (2016) 43 *Journal of Law and Society* 416; and see also the discussion in C. Delage (et al., eds), *Law and New Media: West of Everything* (Edinburgh: Edinburgh University Press, 2019) at ch. 1.
32 *Chambers v DPP*, at 158.
33 For work on AV links to courts and to prisons, see, e.g., the work of Carolyn McKay, *The Pixelated Prisoner: Prison Video Links, Court 'Appearance' and the Justice Matrix* (London: Routledge,

transpires that the legislative sources for determination of the relevant offence predate the invention of Twitter in 2006. More than that, the 2003 Communications Act and its definition of network messages of a 'menacing character' is in fact a simple repetition and legislative incorporation of the 1935 Post Office (Amendment Act) 1935, section 10(2)(a) which 'introduced a prohibition against the misuse of the telephone to communicate indecent, obscene or menacing messages'. Aimed primarily at obscenities directed to individual female exchange telephonists over the wires, the sense of menace indicated by the earlier context and limited technology is clearly and avowedly impertinent to the agon of Twitter. The recirculation of the offence in the 2003 Act simply placed the same menace in the context of what were then new media and rather quaintly depicted by Judge Judge as having 'now advanced to the present electric communications networks'. Passing over the fact that electric communications, meaning the animated, lively, affective tensors of libidinal expression directed on this occasion, as fortuity would have it, to @Crazycolours seems to be precisely what two out of three courts expressly did not want, the landline becomes the juristic cover for jurisliterary invention and for a lawless law.

The bulk of the judgment of Judge Judge is deflective, manipulating the *disposif* of the statutory text to provide the phantasmagoria of legislative provision for what were then non-existent relays. The lengthy, wearisome, boring, and largely irrelevant citation to the Statute, to clauses that are nowhere pertinent to the question of what 'a message of a menacing character' means, section 127(1)(b) and (c) for instance with which the reader is regaled or rather rebuffed serves the purpose of juristic persiflage, distraction from the actual grounds of decision, which are jurisliterary and emerge in paragraph 28 of the judgment. Arriving finally at a discussion of the provenance and purpose of the relevant subsection of 127(1), which is (a), the Judge veers without introduction or explanation, into literature. First, it is political opinion that is cited, the unlikely figure of President Roosevelt is invoked as advocate of 'essential freedoms', what non-English common law would term rights, as including 'freedom of speech and of expression'.[34] Why Judge judges Roosevelt the relevant source, rather than the established jurisprudence of the First Amendment is enigmatic but less to the point

2018); and Michelle Castañeda, 'Virtual Judges in Immigrant Detention: The Mise en Scène of No-show Justice', in Christian Delage, Peter Goodrich and Marco Wan (eds), *Law and New Media: West of Everything* (Edinburgh: Edinburgh University Press, 2019).

34 *Chambers v DPP*, at 156 h–j.

than that the judgment has virulently left the discourse of law for the language and literature of politics as legitimation of the view that '[s]atirical, or iconoclastic, or rude comment, the expression of unpopular or unfashionable opinion about serious or trivial matters, banter or humour, even if distasteful to some or painful to those subjected to it should and no doubt will continue at their customary level, quite undiminished by this legislation'.[35] Which is a peculiar thing to say insofar as it persists in the strategy of the judgment to address everything that the law does not regulate and about which the legislation has nothing to say. It is precisely the gap, the novelty, the lawless escapade and sudden exodus from the lengthily cited, dull and distracting legislative text that is of key interest. In the end it is not even the 1935 Act that triggers decision, but rather Shakespeare.

The actual wording, the absence of quotation marks, integration of the relevant sentence into the judgment, all deserve comment because the role of the drama, *King Lear*, and the meaning of the intervention border on the enigmatic: 'for those who have the inclination to use "Twitter" for the purpose, Shakespeare can be quoted unbowdlerised, and with Edgar, at the end of *King Lear*, they are free to speak not what they ought to say, but what they feel'.[36] Note that Bowdler has lost his capital B, his name, and that the quotation in fact does Bowdlerize both in omitting any context to the quotation, and more significantly in adding 'they', distancing the observation of the times, and then a second time by substituting 'they' for 'we'. The folio edition gives us:

> *Edg.* The weight of this sad time we must obey.
> Speak what we feel, not what we ought to say:
> The oldest hath born most, we that are young,
> Shall never see so much, nor live so long.[37]

The truncated and misquoted reference to *King Lear* is interesting in a dual sense for not doing what it says. As adverted, it Bowdlerises after explicitly stating that it will not do so. And secondly, more symptomatically, it does what legal interpretation most often does, which is to remove the sentence from its dramatic context where the question at issue is that of succession to the Crown upon the death of King Lear:

---

35 Ibid., at 156.
36 Ibid., at 157.
37 Shakespeare, *The Tragedy of King Lear* (London: Herringman, 1685) typography modernized.

> Vex not his Ghost, oh let him pass, he hates him,
> That would upon the rack of this tough World
> Stretch him out longer.

Succession then in the face of treason and death, where the question, as put by Edgar, is 'who has the office?', and who has been 'not vanquish'd. But cozen'd, and beguiled'. All of which is to say that it is the 'sacrifice' of Cordelia, 'the judgment of the Heavens that makes us tremble', the deceptions and dissemblances that led to it, and the honour and duplicity of those that would succeed that are in play and provide the context for the quotation, for speaking what we feel. And that is to speak 'our woe' and befriend those 'that Rule in this Realm'. In other words, it is not enough to steal a phrase, part of a sentence, declarative of the will to express our feelings in the face of the demise of the King's body natural, but the judgment also reads Shakespeare in a manner that mirrors the interpretation of the 2003 Act. Neither text is relevant to the tweet in question, neither law nor 'Shakespeare's law' provides any direct textual resolution.[38] While literature necessarily transports and relays all law, the interesting feature of *DPP v Chambers* is that when the legal text has been recognized, though seldom explicitly, as having run out, literature becomes the legitimation of invention and the vehicle of persuasion.

Judge Judge writes the law and when pressed to self-conscious invention, his authorship of the new rule leans heavily upon Shakespeare, and literature comes quite literally to play the legislative role. It is a self-conscious moment of jurisliterary intervention and signals unequivocally that when law runs out it is fiction, the imaginal, or in this instance Shakespeare's *King Lear* that comes explicitly to legislate determination. While this recourse to a play is transgressive of the boundary of law, it is not that unusual. The *mot juste*, a turn of phrase, maxim or Biblical citation are as we have seen throughout common in common law judgments when the conflict to be decided is charged and when the subject matter of decision is novel and as yet unspoken by precedent or legislation, as was the case here. We witness then an exception which I argue proves the rule, namely that all juristic writing is jurisliterature and recourse to Shakespeare, to the Bible, to Homer or to Jane Austen simply accentuates the rhetorical visibility of the creative process that is generally so carefully hidden

---

38 Though see Desmond Manderson (ed.), '"As If" – the Court of Shakespeare and the Relationship of Law and Literature' (2008) 4 *Law, Culture and the Humanities* 3–69 – Symposium issue.

behind the plethora of citations, quotations, Code and case authorities. Shakespeare marks the moment, the punctum of invention, the sudden insight that a joke, badinage, flirtation from one Twitter handle to another, @Crazycolours, in a short and poorly punctuated tweet, is not a communication of a menacing character.

The dialogic and creative modality of this entry of the Judge into what humanists reference as *circulus disciplinarum*, the play of knowledges, transpires to be the norm, and hence its covert character, its umbrageous status in the enchiridion of law and in the text of judgment. Jurisliterature, the conflation of language and law, literature and legality, imagination and rule, may be most obvious in explicit references to literature and the direct inspiration of creative references but the point is a larger one. Choice of words, language of opening, style of argument, peroration and conclusion are all inventions, plays within and between jurisliterary genres, whether timid or heroic, dry or effulgent. It is in the end always a question of imagination and this can be viewed equally in *DPP v Chambers* in the less striking but nonetheless pertinent apprehension of what the troubled tweet was taken finally to mean. The question is posed as a putatively objective one, not what does 'of a menacing character mean' in subjective terms, and thus, for status, authority and legitimacy: 'whether a message was menacing should be determined by an objective assessment'.[39] This transpires to mean an inductive exercise, an empirical survey of how officials and public subjectively reacted to the tweet, an inquiry into anxiety or its absence in the twittersphere:

> It was posted on 'Twitter' for widespread reading, a conversation piece for the appellant's followers, drawing attention to himself and his predicament ... It seems to us unsurprising, but not irrelevant, that none of those who read the message during the first days after it appeared thought anything of it.[40]

Which is a curious account of objective determination, a reception theory or reader response model of judicial interpretation, although it is evident that the key criterion is that 'it seems to us', to Judge Judge and his brothers, Justices Owen and Griffith Williams. From there to a conclusion is but a short step, a small inference or in fact a repetition of the point: 'on an objective assessment, the decision of the

---
39 *Chambers v DPP*, at 149.
40 Ibid., at 158.

Crown Court that this "tweet" constituted or included a message of a menacing character was not open to it'.[41] It is again a curious point in that it was clearly open to the Crown Court Judge to find the message menacing, as the test is simple and subjective, how does it appear to you, and you, and you, and then by way of extrapolation to 'us'. The High Court is simply preferring, in this rather rare instance, to side with the very vocal twittersphere and to act *pro populi*, and not for 'us' the magistrates and Crown Court judges who begged to differ.

The key point is not the specific subjective assessment of apprehension of menace but rather the jurisliterary process of manifesting decision: from text to twittersphere, from Bench to public opinion, from author of the judgment to auditor of the tweet. Shakespeare is the least of it, a mere symptom of invention and composition which must necessarily move from interior to exterior, both subjectively and in disciplinary genres as well. It is this passage from legal text to social and subjective context that defines authorship and the jurisliterary moment of exploration and experimentation. The boundaries of law and the objectivity of judgment are transgressed time and again, the movement being into theatre, into literature, into theology and philosophy, politics and economics, so as to shore up the abstractions of rule, here a statute based in the regulation of telephonists in 1935, as applicable to virtualities on the internet and the crowd-sourced opinions of microbloggers who virulently protested the conviction of the hapless Chambers caught in his desire for @Crazycolours. The artificiality of the law, itself conceived historically as the predicate of common use, of custom and practice time out of mind, is necessarily an exercise in the fiction of community to which jurisliterature has long contributed and laboured to relay.

To persuade is to move and bend to action and so the final category is that of performance, the *legis actio* that gives effect to the persuasive argument as incorporated into the judgment. The decision is the cut, the scythe of judgment, and it is what matters matterphorically, meaning as outcome and distributor of the fate of those bodies, entities, concepts and variegated forms of persons who came before the law. Effect, as Agamben elaborates, is the doing that is the result of determination, the new meaning that is generated and enacted through the liturgical process of trial, verdict and juristic decision. This is the transfer that occasions change and which is the reason for fiction, the cause of

---

41 Ibid., at 159.

the jurisliterary role in the elaboration and transmission of the legal form of life as our contested yet obligatory collective *modus vivendi* or national manner of being. Matterphor as the concrete morphology of meaning and as the effect of extended allegory, as the radical and material performativity of *allegoresis* has in law to find an ending, a terminus in decision. Literature again will play the law and enforce, which is to say give effect to the interpretation that has resulted in the determination.

There is an easy and intriguing instance of this, stated by way of dissenting judgment, with the clarity and precision of disbelief, by no less an authority than Lord Atkin in a case concerning the exercise of a power under section 18(b) of the 1939 Defence Powers Regulations.[42] This allowed the Secretary of State to order the detention of anyone whom he 'has reasonable cause to believe ... to be of hostile origin or associations or to have been recently concerned in acts prejudicial to the public safety or the defence of the realm or in the preparation or instigation of such acts ...'. The majority, citing to the liberty of the subject, to Magna Carta, to inalienable freedoms, then went on to decide in favour of the Secretary of State, and took section 18(b) to also have the meaning, if the Secretary of State 'believes the thing in question'. Lord Atkin rebelled. The Secretary must have reasonable cause to believe on the basis of external or objective facts. Cicero is cited in inverted form in support of his view, to the effect that '[i]n this county, amid the clash of arms, the laws are not silent'.[43] Armed then with the sound and fury of laws, Lord Atkin acts with withering effect, pronouncing of Viscount Maugham's majority interpretation:

> I know of only one authority which might justify the suggested method of construction: 'When I use a word,' Humpty Dumpty said in rather a scornful tone, 'it means just what I choose it to mean, neither more nor less.' 'The question is,' said Alice, 'whether you can make words mean so many different things.' 'The question is,' said Humpty Dumpty, 'which is to be master — that's all.' ('Through the Looking Glass,' c. vi.) After all this long discussion the question is whether the words 'If a man has' can mean 'If a man thinks he has.' I am of opinion that they cannot . . .

In the boldest of terms, through the looking glass, in the alternate or fictive narrative of law, words mean what sovereigns, judges, and here

---
42 *Liversidge v Sir John Anderson* (1941) AC 206.
43 Ibid., at 244, the reference is to the Latin maxim, *silent enim leges inter arma*.

literary and poetic authorities dictate that they mean. It is an old message in the sense that early modern lawyers were well aware that intendment, the narrative being relayed, the transfer of meaning directed towards auditor or reader determines content. Thus Swinburne, to take an early modern practitioner orientated example, asks: 'what are words but messengers of men's minds? And wherefore serve tongues, but to express men's meanings?' If the words fail to manifest the intent then the words must be emended.[44] Such is what the majority, in Lord Atkin's view, has done, and they have in this instance failed the words because no other meaning than that expressed could legally have been intended.

The incursion of *Alice* into the juridical text and interpretation is not unusual, in that the narrative of law has constantly to be updated and the Republic of Lawyers needs to open its doors to the next generation of personnel, their culture and language. Matter moves, and meaning is transferred, a point which is made most directly by Lord Rogers of Earlsferry in a case concerned with whether homosexual cohabitants could be 'spouses' within the meaning of the Rent Act.[45] He decided that they could, that the legislative use of the expression had changed in meaning, that a different narrative was now to be told, and invokes the famously gay poet and literary critic A.E. Housman in support of his conclusion:

> When Housman addressed the meeting of the Classical Association in Cambridge in 1921, he reminded them that the key to the sound emendation of a corrupt text does not lie in altering the text by changing one letter rather than half a dozen words. The key is that the emendation must start from careful consideration of the writer's thought.[46]

Time, the sedimentation of value, corrupts the past meaning and the word morphoses along with changing customs and *mores*. The literalist claim to univocity of subject and expression fissures into plurality because it is inadequate to the implicit or here express transfer of meaning that occurs in all legal actions, in each new expression. What is surprising is simply the directness of acknowledgement that the seamless web of law is constantly being redrawn, enacted, changed and

---

44 Henry Swinburne, *A Treatise of Spousals, or Matrimonial Contracts* (London: Browne, 1686) at 63–4.

45 *Ghaidan v Godin-Mendoza* [2004] UKHL 30, [2004] 3 All ER 411.

46 *Ghaidan*, [2004] 3 All ER 411 at 454 [para 122].

expanded. The verdict is not simply the truth as found and spoken by jury or fact finder, it is also, at the level of doctrine, the novel matter, the neoteric narrative and new meaning that the judgment inscribes into law. The consequence, the liturgical *effectus* or putting into practice, be it *stasis* or revolution, is the point of material change and performance.

In the celebrated or notorious decision in *Investor's Compensation Scheme*, it was not a word, not even a comma, but a perilunar parenthesis that was in dispute.[47] The issue concerned an assignment of actions that included an exclusion of '[a]ny claim (whether sounding in rescission for undue influence or otherwise) . . .' The trial Judge, the double-barreled Evans-Lombe J. decided that this meant that the beneficiary of the exclusion had retained the right to bring a claim for rescission. The parenthetical was in effect to be shifted four words further forward so that any claim for rescission was what was retained, and the parenthesis helped define the species of rescission. In the Court of Appeals, Legatt LJ impugned the first instance determination as doing violence to the words of the instrument and claiming a meaning that was not available. Like Humpty Dumpty in *Through the Looking Glass*, the lowlier Court was making words mean what they wanted them to mean. The reference is to Humpty Dumpty pointing out that there are 364 days in the year when you might get unbirthday presents:

> 'Certainly', said Alice.
> 'And only one for birthday presents, you know. There's glory for you!'
> 'I don't know what you mean by "glory",' Alice said.
> Humpty Dumpty smiled contemptuously. 'Of course you don't—till I tell you. I meant "there's a nice knock-down argument for you!"'
> 'But "glory" doesn't mean "a nice knock-down argument",' Alice objected.
> 'When *I* use a word', Humpty Dumpty said, in rather a scornful tone, 'it means just what I choose it to mean—neither more nor less'.

In the House of Lords, Lord Hoffmann sides with Humpty Dumpty, and earlier Henry Swinburne. Where the words do not reflect the intention, then the words must be emended. It is not, however, the instrument that is my primary concern, but rather the judicial exchanges which move then to a *topos* of domestic felines and a hypothetical lease that excludes 'any pets (whether neutered Persian cats or otherwise).' This in turn is likened to Mrs Malaprop saying that '[s]he is as obstinate as an allegory on the banks of the Nile'. These, Lord Hoffmann suggests,

---

47 *Investor's Compensation Scheme v West Bromwich Building Soc.* [1998] 1 All E.R. 98.

are all slips, symptoms of a split subject, signs of desire frustrated in expression. Mrs Malaprop, as Lord Hoffmann expounds her case in an earlier decision, conveys her meaning unambiguously through the use of the wrong words:

> When she says 'She is as obstinate as an allegory on the banks of the Nile', we reject the conventional or literal meaning of allegory as making nonsense of the sentence and substitute 'alligator' by using our background knowledge of the things likely to be found on the banks of the Nile and choosing one which sounds rather like 'allegory'.[48]

Ironically, however, Lord Hoffmann has in fact indicated that Mrs Malaprop is far from having used the wrong words because according to him she has made perfect sense. The allegory in question, in his view, is of alligators, a double transfer or *allegoresis* whereby Mrs Malaprop is transported to the banks of the Nile and allegories become alligators. For Lord Hoffmann the portmanteau word that should have been produced from his analysis would be allegatory.

What is in issue is the production of sense which is always and necessarily triggered, as in Lord Hoffmann's two examples, by nonsense, a term that Deleuze usefully defines as 'excess of meaning . . . it is that which . . . enacts the donation of sense . . .'.[49] We construct meaning, and nonsense is the plenitude and plethora, the exuberance of possibilities contained in the words and most especially in their relations to each other. Allegory is a perfectly conventional word and an allegory on the banks of the Nile, obstinate or pliable, is, as the learned Judge could have pointed out, a rhetorical *catachresis*, meaning a seemingly improper use which in time becomes an accepted meaning. We are comfortable now with allegories on the banks of the Nile and once we move beyond Lord Hoffmann's desire to correct a perceived corruption, we can recognize that this instance is itself an allegory of meaning production, a donation of sense as Deleuze defines it. Allegory is obstinate. It is precisely its obduracy and persistence that moves language on, that drives discourse, that in changing sense generates new sensibilities.

---

48 *Mannai Investment v Eagle Star Life Assurance Co Ltd* [1997]3 All ER 352, at 375.
49 Gilles Deleuze, *The Logic of Sense* (London: Athlone, 1990) at 71.

4 Legal imaginations

The figures of law, matterphor and metaphor, ranging from vivified divinities to haunted houses and speaking eggs, *King Lear* to *Alice in Wonderland*, are the modes of transfer, the figures of dissemination and change of meaning. The persuasive force of law, the avenues of its affective appeal lie in these jurisliterary formulae, the most visible points of intersection between legal discourse and its various audiences, professional and public, pedagogic and popular. In the language of classical rhetoric these figures of speech – specifically *enargeia* or *ekphrasis* – operate precisely to make arguments visible, to bring the actors and action clearly before the eyes of the auditor and lector. The appeal to the senses is primarily to sight as the most direct path to persuasion. As the author of the *Rhetorica ad Herennium* puts it, 'demonstration is to express things in words and . . . to put things before the eyes so that they can be seen'.[1] For Quintilian, following Cicero, the figure is that of ocular demonstration which moves beyond mere mention of action, and 'proceeds to show how it was done . . . in full detail'. This is elsewhere termed vivid illustration and also *visiones* meaning 'appealing to the eyes rather than the ears', so as to imagine in pictorial aspect the acts and actors at play. Quintilian gives the example of: 'He came into the forum on fire with criminal madness: his eyes blazed and cruelty was written in every feature of his countenance.'[2] A jurisliterary example in which the force of depiction drives the advocacy of the cause. More than that the portrayal of insane and unbounded threat attacks the senses and mobilizes an affective response that precedes rational deliberation. As Simonides, according to Plutarch, formulated it, poetry is talking painting, entry into sense and scene.[3]

---

1 *Ad Herennium*, 4.55.68 *Demonstratio est cum ita uerbis res exprimitur . . . et res ante oculos esse uideatur.*
2 Quintilian, *Institutio oratoria* book 9.2.40.
3 Plutarch, *Moralia*, 346F.

What is most evident, even in these early rhetorical depictions of legal discourse, is that the jurisliterary appeal to the imaginal is in full consonance with the theological tracts which frequently reiterated the power and the danger of the image as the most immediate transport of will and affections. The terminology of the rhetoricians is corporeal and theatrical. The task is to act out the events depicted so that they come before the eyes, so that they trigger emotion, which is to say performativity, movement, the drama of sensible engagement. The image bends the will to action and as recent studies of cinema and new media confirm, the image is not only more than it seems, it slips past conscious screening and renders its effect prior to thought. There is a prevalence of shark aesthetics, a competition to impact viewers and attract audiences with vivid and often shocking imagery that will generate powerful affective reactions and so attract attention and followings. This transition to the legal videosphere, to an imaginal relay of legal presences and practices lowers the cathartic impact of court and trial amongst the plethora of other, equally fictive courts and trials.[4] While some view this phenomenon of an image driven public sphere as a negative, as irrational and populist, there is also a dimension of potential and opportunity which can be illustrated by the example of the theatre of law and specifically the increasing use of film, animatrix, and imagery in the relay of precedent and the practice of lawyers. As the medium changes, so too does the law.[5] In transition lies opportunity and in this instance the imaginal, an image driven videosphere proffers that change in perspective that accompanies non-linear modes of thinking, of habitus and sensibility.

Prior to thought we have first to imagine. As the art historian Didi-Huberman has lengthily expounded, this priority of the image is the

---

4 For an interesting history of this transition, see Gabriele Pedullà, *In Broad Daylight: Movies and Spectators after the Cinema* (London: Verso, 2012). On the imaginal character of virtual imagery, see also Chiara Bottici, *Imaginal Politics* (New York: Columbia University Press, 2015). In a juristic context, see Desmond Manderson (ed.), *Law and the Visual: Representations, Technologies, Critique* (Toronto: University of Toronto Press, 2018); Christian Delage, Peter Goodrich and Marco Wan (eds), *Law and New Media: West of Everything* (Edinburgh: Edinburgh University Press, 2019).

5 A point well made in terms of the classical trinity, *ordo, lex, medium,* in Régis Debray, *Cours de médiologie générale* (Paris: Gallimard, 1995) at 321–5. What is at issue for Debray is the transmission of the *certum*, of which he goes on to point out that in the videosphere 'a certitude that is not visible, that is not sensible, is no longer a certitude.' (at 323) For the anglophone, there is are translations of some of Debray's shorter works, such as *Media Manifestos: On the Technological Transmission of Cultural Forms* (London: Verso, 1996); *Transmitting Culture* (New York: Columbia University Press, 2004).

starting point, the transition to thinking, the opening of the viewer to the opening of the viewed.[6] Our tendency, particularly juristically, is to immobilize the image, to treat it *ex post facto* as a dead thing, a mere representation of a static or filmed scene. The depiction is viewed as a capture and incarceration of what is viewed, a closed and unchanging portrait of person, thing or event as external to, and without relation to the viewer. To open the image, for Didi-Huberman, is to open to it and engage with it as a living, ambulatory, historical and changing form that exists transiently in relation to the active gaze that unlocks it and is opened up by it.[7] What this means in terms of jurisliterature is that the opening of legal texts to the use of images, the increasing importance of imagery not only as evidence, but now also as part of adversarial argument and of the judicial reasoning of decisions increasingly invokes a more expansively humanistic and diversely aesthetic approach to law's transmission. The literary criticism of law that was advocated by James Boyd White some 45 years ago, and by Weisberg and Binder, now two decades ago, has significant jurisliterary purchase but requires expansion to include text and image, description and pictorial depictions, maxims and emblems.[8]

Moving directly to the new technologies of transmission and relay of law, it is clear that the old conception of the text as a linear, scriptural and bounded item stored in carefully guarded archives and libraries no longer obtains. The performative dimension of law, its materiality and geopolitical embeddedness is increasingly visible at the same time that the internet fragments and disperses the forms of its relay. The result is a dissipation and pluralization of the media of dissemination, a fragmentation and scintillation of law's social presence and performances in that it becomes accessible in partial forms, exciting social media attention and microblogging at the same time as it morphs in modality, becoming available in visual and imaginal modes, in bytes, tweets, as also Instagram, photograms, screenshots, film clips and all the other diverse relays of the imaginal that begins, of course, in Christian traditions, with the Word as the all-encompassing, ultra-juridical sign of a Deity who always spoke in visible forms, through burning bushes, clouds, tablets of stone, through his own image, Christ, and then in Pentecostal mode through the ambulant images of the disciples. The

---

6 George Didi-Huberman, *L'Image ouverte* (Paris: Gallimard, 2003).
7 George Didi-Huberman, *The Eye of History* (Cambridge, MA: MIT, 2016).
8 Guyora Binder and Robert Weisberg, *Literary Criticisms of Law* (Princeton: Princeton University Press, 2000) at ch. 1.

sacraments, in theological argot are *verba visibilia*, visible words, and the book too was also used in many ceremonies and rites as a physical object and tactile form. It is that emboldened sense of the materiality and performativity of signs which needs to be recollected so as to acknowledge the essential materiality of the word while also recognizing and mobilizing the necessary correlation and imbrication of the verbal and the visible, of story and sensibility, reason and affect as complements not opposites.

Lawyers, like theologians, have long been aware of the priority of images in pedagogy and persuasion. To allure and attach a subject to the legal institution, to teach and to train, is a question initially of affect and image, and so of inculcating a sense of the world. We start with pictures. The image instructs, illustrates and illuminates, a feature of law that the jurists have long been aware of, although rather unwilling to divulge or share. Thus Justinian in the *Institutes* begins with the declaration that 'the Emperor should not only be armed with laws, but also decorated with arms' – *Imperatoriam maiestatem non solum armis decoratam, sed etiam legibus oportet esse armatam.* The key lies in the decoration with arms and the arming with laws, these are striking figures of sovereign power, but also images that we carry in us unconsciously, as oneiric mnemonics. The psychoanalytic jurist Pierre Legendre makes this point at length in recuperating the etymology of the first sentence of the *Institutes* and specifically the connotations of *decor* and *decorum*, as dream images, and also as signifying beauty, elegance, charm and grace.[9] These are how the legislator fascinates and binds, how the jurist gets under the skin and governs the unconscious in the name of the father, through a paternal law. Such is the Freudian theory and finds significant juristic support in the early modern use of legal emblems, printed woodcut pictures in books by jurists as also in doctrinal legal texts where pictures would play the role of maxims, and provide the dogmatic ground of rules. The Senneton edition of the *Corpus iuris civilis* from 1550, remarks in its prefatory discussion that 'we wanted the whole body of the book and its titles to be decorated with elegant images, so that the grounds of the things written, can be represented to the eyes, as if living'.[10] In the preface to the first volume of the *Digest*, the decorative function of the images is again mentioned

---

9 Pierre Legendre, *L'Empire de la vérité: Introduction aux espaces dogmatiques industriels* (Paris: Fayard, 1983) 25–34. For discussion of this theme, see Goodrich, *Legal Emblems and the Art of Law* (Cambridge: Cambridge University Press, 2014) at ch 8.

10 *Institutiones quæ sunt civilis iuris elementa* (Senneton: Lyon, 1550) the full passage is: *'totius*

in a wording close to that of Justinian, stating that the text will be 'decorated with images and adorned with emblematic pictures'.[11]

Juristically the use of the verb to decorate references an aesthetic of transmission but its stronger sense is that of conveying honour, hierarchy, the office and dignity of the rules elaborated. The images are the foundation of the legal order, the illumination of sources conveying the bedrock of the juridical institution as ordained by both divine and human knowledge. This, in sport and stumble, is the dream of normativity, the wish fulfilment of the author of the laws, the phantasmagoria that will occupy the nocturnal perambulations of the subject's sleeping body. The aesthetic of law, the fascination and dream like quality of rites and ceremonies, spectacles and images, are not incidents but rather fundaments of the juridical, the building blocks of the institution, its notes of dignity that convey in a direct and visible fashion the offices and *dramatis personae* of governance as dignitaries, the temporary holders of timeless offices, inhabitants of institutions that do not die. The image is in this sense the *corpus mysticum* of the state, and in common law terms it is the unwritten dimension of custom and use from time out of mind.[12] The image precedes and exceeds the word, it captures the child and governs the adult. It is the interior of legality, the depiction that drives and the face that frames the rule of law.

The exercise in history, the recuperation of a sense of the emblem as a lawful depiction, and of the visual notes of dignity as the markers of the law of images – *ius imaginum* – is important to ground the juridical frame and meaning of the current transition to virtual and imaginal relays of legality. The juridical person is a legal fiction, an image both literally and figuratively and it is this sense of the theatre of justice and truth that the tradition harbours as one of the key *arcana imperii* or mysteries of state. The jurisliterary appeal to legal elegance, to the beauty of juridical reason, and to the virtues of illustration and illumination, décor and decorum, fiction and figure, provides both a method

---

corpus librū, et libri prototitlon decorari voluimus eleganti imagine pista, quæ rei scriptæ hypothesin, quasi vitam, ab oculus repræsentat.'

11 Cited in the excellent Valérie Hayaert, 'Emblems', in Stern et al. (eds), *The Oxford Handbook of Law and Humanities* (Oxford: Oxford University Press, 2020) at 761: '*per imagines decoratus et mythicis emblematum picturis illustratum.*'

12 The *corpus mysticum* references the undying body of the sovereign as ably propounded by Ernst Kantorowicz, *The King's Two Bodies: A Study in Medieval Political Theology* [1957] (Princeton: Princeton University Press, 2016). On the semiotics of time out of mind, see Peter Goodrich, *Languages of Law* (London: Weidenfeld & Nicolson, 1992) at ch 6.

and a trajectory for the current turn to the use of images in the diverse practices of lawyers and their iterations of law. The camera tells stories in pictures and words, and increasingly the direction and governance of the social is by means of visual as well as verbal *allegoresis*. The lens paints a picture with words and images, colour and sound, motion and emotion creating a novel epistemic issue for lawyers. How is the jurist to utilize and optimize the incursion of imagery in the practice and reasoning of law? More than that, as Cornelia Vismann expanded the question, the camera both brings the world into the courtroom but also, despite the jealous efforts of judges to use the doctrine of contempt of court to prevent the escape of unauthorized images onto the internet, the law inevitably fails: 'The camera intervenes in even the forensic ritual of coding violence and threatens to topple the media conversion of act to language in favor of another: act to image.'[13] The photographing, filming, and blogging of the *in camera* by the omnipresent mobile optimized computer and phone cameras bleeds out of court and drags the juridical into the social despite the best efforts and rearguard protestations of a judiciary that is only slowly learning to accommodate the novel media.

The narrative, the allegory, is also in pictures and as we now know well, the images impact first and hardest, setting the frame, sticking in memory, moving to action.[14] Vismann makes the point that once the camera is in court, the nature of the legal process changes because the audience has exponentially expanded. The theatrical closure in terms of time, space, and action has exploded and the courts are increasingly aware, as is the profession, that much of the significance of rule and judgment has not only escaped the library, but is now out of court, in the news, media and streaming services which channel and convey the social presence of law on the internet. As Sherwin puts it, law goes pop, rule is digital, and visual persuasion carries the norm away.[15] The legal issue is most frequently that of how to control the circulation and use of imagery and hence to restrict access to it, and interpretations of it. In reviewing attempts to constrain access and channel practices

---

13 Cornelia Vismann, 'Tele-Tribunals: Anatomy of a Medium' (2003) 10 *Grey Room* 5, 15.
14 For an account of the didactic and mnemonic value of images, see the excellent Susanna Berger, *The Art of Philosophy: Visual Thinking in Europe from the Late Renaissance to the Early Enlightenment* (Princeton: Princeton University Press, 2017).
15 Richard Sherwin, one of the pioneers of visual legal studies, has expounded his views most systematically in Sherwin, *When Law Goes Pop: The Vanishing Line Between Law and Popular Culture* (Chicago: Chicago University Press, 2000); and in Sherwin, *Visualizing Law in the Age of the Digital Baroque: Arabesques and Entanglements* (London: Routledge, 2012).

of interpretation or, better, apprehension of juristic images, it will be evident that the judiciary in particular has a very limited critical comprehension of the potential novelty of the medium, the diversification of meaning that it introduces and the affective quality and scope of its impact.

The tension between justice being visible and control of cameras in court, as also of the media and means of showing law in action, can be seen most directly in the law of contempt of court. Appearance in court and the appearance of the court are heavily regulated. A juror wearing a T-shirt with 'FCUK FAME' on it was expelled from the court for what the Judge deemed to be a, presumably dyslexic, expletive. In a US court, a defendant who when he turned to leave the court was seen by the Judge to have 'I fuck like a beast' on the back of his T-Shirt was sanctioned. Defendants in a defamation suit in Singapore who stood outside court wearing T-Shirts with pictures of a kangaroo in judicial robes were fined and sentenced to imprisonment. So far so good, sartorial propriety is part of the ceremonial function of the court, and persons not clothes should apparently or apparel to speak. The players should have their costumes for their parts, that of member of the public included. This does not, however, explain the restrictions upon filming or photographing what occurs in court. If the public has a right to attend and view proceedings, then in an age of virtual relay and viral dissemination it should be possible to take and circulate images of what has taken place. The Supreme Court of the UK is now permanently filmed but visitors to courts who film or photograph still face sanctions for contempt of court and punishment for posting these images on the web. The rule dates back to the 1925 Criminal Justice Act which by section 4(1) stipulates that no person shall '(a) take or attempt to take in any court any photograph, or with a view to publication make or attempt to make in any court any portrait or sketch of any person being a judge of the court or a juror or a witness in or a party to any proceedings before the court, whether civil or criminal'.

The statute was an attempt to protect and isolate the proceedings in court from criticism that might demit from the aura of juristic sanctity and the ceremonial valence of proceedings. At the root of the legislation lay the 1912 Old Bailey case of *R v Frederick Henry Seddon and Margaret Ann Seddon*, in which an observer had secretly photographed the Judge, with a black cap over his wig, and a priest beside him, pronouncing the death penalty on the first defendant (Figure 4.1 below). This was published in the *Daily Mail* and led to 'an enormous public

74 ADVANCED INTRODUCTION TO LAW AND LITERATURE

Source: https://www.msn.com/en-nz/news/photos/the-drama-of-the-courtroom-rare-pictures-taken-from-inside-the-docks-before-photographers-were-banned-in-1925/ss-BBGgWwC?fullscreen=true#image=2

Figure 4.1 *R v Frederick Henry Seddon* – public domain

outcry at [the] trial's verdict; and a petition bearing more than 250,000 signatures claiming [Seddon's] innocence'.[16] The photograph let the secret of law slip out of the courtroom and showed the performative moment of judicial killing *in actu*, or going down. The bare black and white image relays the pomp and the abstraction of the legal ritual, the elevated throne with its royal emblem, the wigs, gowns and costumes, the bar, the piles of books, the papers, and then spatial arrangements of this theatrical staging, the well of the court looking up to the bench, the segregation of the accused, the jury benches, all contributing to the seriously hierarchical semiotics of the courtroom. As one study of photography and law usefully formulates it:

> the literalism of the photograph challenged the real meaning of capital punishment as being about abstractions and ideas of justice and showed it as the act of killing an actual human being. It can therefore be seen that a combination of the photographic form and a legal outsider's vision appeared to merge as a challenge to the existing legal institution and dominant ideas of legal truth.[17]

The picture of the performance of the death penalty was provocative and triggered a popular campaign against the decision and by association in condemnation of the law. It was thus the view of those promoting the

---

16 Geoffrey Howse, *Murder and Mayhem in North London* (Barnsley: Wharncliffe Books, 2010), 78.
17 Suneel Mehmi, *Fiction and the Reaction to Photography: Literalism, the Law and the Conditions and the Control of Reading from the Invention of Photography to the 1920s* (London: Routledge, 2021).

ban on photographs and courtroom sketches that too much had been seen and the authorized narrative of juridical reason had come undone in the maelstrom of public perception and opination. It appears that the narrative must be controlled and the proximity, accessibility and affective visibility of pictorial representations wrests the story to be told from the chirograph of the lawyers. The acclamatory discourse of law, its fusion with liturgy and worship, was fractured through exposure.

In a more recent but comparable example, in *Solicitor General v Cox and Parker Stokes*, the first respondent, a friend of the defendant in a murder trial took five photographs and video with his phone camera: 'Some images show dock officers. Some images, and the video, include part of the notices prohibiting the use of mobile phones.'[18] Other photographs were of the Judge and the courtroom. The second respondent uploaded the images to Facebook and later uploaded a picture of the Judge with negative comments. The first respondent later also uploaded the picture of the Judge, HHJ Picton, to his own Facebook page. In finding the defendants guilty of contempt, the Judge bemoans the difficulties that the courts face in controlling social media and goes on to remark:

> The course of conduct here was very serious. In the one case, the use of a photograph taken in contempt of court as glorification of a murderer; in the other case, a gross piece of abuse of a judge following upon taking a photograph in contempt. In each case they may properly be seen together, given the close relationship between the two respondents and the murderer, and they are an intended demonstration of gang loyalty, and of defiance of the court and of this murder case, in particular.[19]

Amongst the many intriguing features of this statement is the relationship between words and images. The Court and the Judge have appeared in public, on Facebook after the sentencing hearing was completed. The defendants had posted pictures of the court, of some signage, and of the defendant and the Judge amongst other personnel. These pictures depict the inside of the building, some features of it, and participants in it. The photograph itself can hardly be deemed contemptuous, it shows what it shows, a sitting Judge, while the words, written out of court, free of appearance and apparel in court, are not of themselves sanctionable now that the offence of scandalizing the

---

18 *Her Majesty's Solicitor General v Cox and Parker Stokes* [2016] EWCH 1241 (QB).
19 *Cox and Parker Stokes* at para. 6.

Source: https://www.dailymail.co.uk/news/article-1018393/Judge-lifts-thugs-curfew--golfing-holiday.html. Used with permission of John Hawkins, Gloucestershire News Service

Figure 4.2 *His Honour Justice Picton*

court has been judicially abolished.[20] It is precisely the transition from act to image that is in issue and dispute. The self-image of the Court has been challenged, the licit portrait of proceedings fractured by the respondents and the precarious dignity of the juridical institution and invested personnel has been criticized and contested. The photograph takes what is inside the law too far outside the juridical institution, into the world and its unfamiliarities.

The image appears to be something of an Achilles' heel for the court, a moment of hysterical blindness insofar as the image of HHJ Picton

---

20 See *Ahnee v Director of Public Prosecutions* [1999] 2 AC 294. As the Court of Appeal puts it in *Re Yaxley-Lennon* [2019] 1 All ER 594 at 604 d: 'criminal contempts are those which broadly involve acts that threaten the administration of justice'. In *Dhooharika v DPP* [2014] UKPC 11, the Court cites Lord Justice Simon Brown with approval: 'a wry smile is, I think, our usual response and the more extravagant the allegations, the more ludicrous they sound'.

can be and frequently is reproduced in the Press and subjected to criticism – Figure 4.2 here taken from the front page of the *Daily Mail*, with an article highly critical of a decision he had made, though lacking expletives.[21] Picton is pictured often enough, and the prohibition or labelling such pictures contempt of court suffers from a superficiality of viewing and a lack of any critical apparatus which would account for the photogram depicting the Judge as dependent upon the abuse or other commentary that accompanies its posting. It is certainly hard to see the photograph as glorifying murder and so the analysis in the end has to fall back upon the simple fact of taking a photograph in a courthouse that has posted a sign prohibiting photographs of a process that is supposed to be open to and viewable by the public at large. The inside of the court is appearing out of court, in pictures both licit and illicit. It is happening and it will continue to happen in increasing forms and augmented occasions. Rather than endeavouring to censor, contain and punish such viral presence, tolerance and a more sophisticated understanding of the competing narratives and differing montages of the juridical as an acceleratingly imaginal concatenation of phenomena is the necessary task of jurisliterary imagination. The viserbal is now a necessary part of the relay of law, visual and verbal, text and image, words mingling with pictures.

The question at issue in *Cox* is that of the mutable and changing status of the images in issue. Does the text alter the image? Does the photograph belie the text? The judicial interpretation of the image is one that reduces it to the written commentary, as if the pictures lack autonomy, are immobile and transparent, to be read and not viewed. Compare that case of pictures getting out of court to an Australian case in which the Judge takes a photograph that he brings into the court. Narrative in a curiously ambiguous sense of stories and storeys comes into intriguing play in *Clare and Others v Bedelis*. The issue was one of a restrictive covenant upon land, by which purchasers of land were prohibited from 'erecting any dwelling house other than one having walls of brick or stone and being not more than one storey in height'.[22] A 52-page judgment ensues, primarily on the question of what is a storey, and then what is a brick. It follows in a lengthy line of cases of ontological as well as epistemic definition of issues such as what is a roof,[23] what is a

---

21 'Judge lifts thug's curfew – so he can go on a golfing holiday', *Daily Mail* 6 May 2008.
22 *Clare and Ors v Eva Bedelis* [2016] VSC 381 at 4 para. 17.
23 On what is a roof, see *Health Service Executive v Brookshore Ltd* [2010] IEHC 165, at para. 1.

building,[24] what is a 'building site',[25] what is a 'dwelling house',[26] what is a floor,[27] and similar architectural conundrums, and the answer comes with a judicial excursion both literal and metaphoric: 'An image of a subject often conveys a meaning more effectively than a description. The picture below was taken by me on Friday 17 June 2016. The house depicted is, in my view, not more than one story [sic] in height'.[28] (Figure 4.3 opposite) The story at issue in the case is one of height and dimension as well as of interpretation of the purpose of the covenant and in that context the picture is somewhat surprising. It is not that the judge himself took the photograph. It is not that the Judge, having taken and put the photograph in evidence, simply says that it is 'in my view', according that is to the photograph that he took, not more than one storey although the insertion of my view and my picture does personalize the perspective. What is significant and now very common is that there is no further analysis of the image. Here the house photographed is the issue and so the story of whether it is one storey or not requires, if it is to be visually determined as the Judge evidently desires, some account of what is seen, as opposed to the bare assertion that 'he', His Honour Associate Justice David Mark Brudenell Derham, views it as one storey when what he has photographed is clearly, as digitally captured, on the right side, two storeys, albeit on an incline. The photograph transpires in fact to be entirely misleading, and his perceptual remark unhelpful in deciding because it shows an irrelevant view and perspective upon the house.

Tucked away, secreted, almost hidden at the end of the judgment is a plan of the properties subject to the restrictive covenant, the lots being outlined in blue. The house at issue is shaded in yellow, and is on the incline which the photograph indicates as sloping down from Yvonne Court toward Halcyon Drive. What is significant about the Plan shown is that it indicates that the covenant is to protect the view from behind the building so that Waverly Glen retains an unimpeded vista of a panoramic horizon. The photograph from the front of the house thus provides no direct evidence of whether one or more storeys are visible from the rear. A map with contour lines, tabulation of eleva-

---

24 *R (on the Application of Ghai) v Newcastle City Council* [2009] EWHC 978 (Admin).
25 *Clark v Wodehouse* 669 P.2d 101 (1983).
26 *Downie v Lockwood* [1965] VR 257.
27 *Leichhardt Municipal Council v Daniel Callaghan Pty Ltd* (1981) 46 LGRA 29 (holding that a floor is a storey).
28 *Clare and Ors* at 34 para. 84.

LEGAL IMAGINATIONS 79

Source: https://restrictivecovenants.files.wordpress.com/2016/07/2016-07-07-orders-merits-clare-ors-v-bedelis-2016-vsc-381.pdf

Figure 4.3 *Clare and Ors v Eva Bedelis*

tion and view would be necessary for a properly visual or adequately depicted representation of the issue to be determined. There are other questions at issue, such as whether the garage is within the definition of a dwelling house and so to be counted in the vertical ascension of the property. The Judge also poses a hypothetical, that of whether the property would be deemed two storeys if rather than a garage there were simply piers or pillars without walls and open to the elements holding the latter portion of the property level with the rest of the dwelling.

The Judge, to his credit, or by inadvertence, we cannot say, shows the photograph of that aspect of the house least favourable to his determination and most likely to be viewed as two storeys. More to the point, however, the photograph is viewed as transparent, it is simply deemed to be what it shows without any account of apparatus, perspective, choice of exposure, focus, resolution, field of view, angle, height and all of the other facets of framing, scanning and locating that make up the composite of this *dispositif* or close up of the face of a house. This, however, is the judicial method of apprehending, proffering a reading of the surfaces of images, the story and in this case also the storey that they wish to tell. Returning to the judgment, the judicial apprehension of the purpose of viewing is significant: 'It is impossible to construe this, or any, covenant, in a completely abstract way.' In a spirit not far removed from the new materialism, the approach is one which refuses to countenance an abstract or in jurisprudential argot 'purely' theoretical analysis. 'It cannot be done in the abstract', the Judge reiterates, it is a question of construction that requires context, factual assessment, purpose, topography, lie of the land, neighbourhood, the nature and physical characteristics of the housing in the vicinity, and most important of all, the repeatedly used term, 'my view'. Part of the question is posed as that of how these factors will impact 'any dwelling house that can, sensibly, be built on the Land'.[29] There is, in other words, no literal meaning to the word storey in the covenant. The decision has to be particular.

The photograph then is a very partial view of the building and offers no dispositive information as to whether the restrictive covenant has been breached. The Judge in fact acknowledges that it is not directly pertinent to the questions to be resolved:

> the house under construction on the Land, and the house it replaced, has only a single level in that part of the house to the rear, on the southern side, of the lot. Thus, whether or not there is a sub floor at the front of the lot facing Yvonne Court will not have any impact on the properties to the south.[30]

There is acknowledgment as well of another apprehension and inspection of the property and its context in relation to the meaning of 'brick or stone':

> In my unaccompanied view of the Land and neighbourhood, it became apparent that the bulk of the houses were constructed with an external appearance of brick ... the overall appearance of the neighbourhood was that the houses were substantial in size and built of brick whether that was solid brick or brick veneer could not be seen.[31]

In both cases, what is seen is not what is at issue and in dispute. The subject of determination is invisible. The height of the building is of relevance only from the rear, which is not photographed, and the

---

29 Ibid., at para. 69.
30 Ibid., at para. 36 d.
31 Ibid., at para. 112.

material used for construction of the building is not photographed although the Judge does indicate that he has, in an unaccompanied manner, conducted a visual inspection of the neighbourhood and buildings but cannot discern if the brick used is veneer or solid. So why report viewings that provide non-probative impressions, and why post a photograph that is of something other than the view necessary to deciding if the restrictive covenant has been infracted?

The answer lies in the legal history of the image, the *ius imaginum*, which dictates that the pictorial depiction is an end point, the *non plus ultra* where questioning terminates in the screening of the void with the image. Borrowing from Pierre Legendre, 'the image is the dogma' because it is that which requires no authorization beyond its own manifestation. This means that the image represents what is not there, it is in theological terms the trace of an absence, the materialization of an immaterial being. The classic trinity is that of *vestigium, imago, similitudo* – vestige, image, likeness.[32] The paradox of the Judge's inquiry into the height of the house is thus twofold. First, he inserts a photograph that he has taken on an excursion. The photograph is a vestige of the building, a materialization in a virtual form of something that is not present. The depiction presences absence, manifesting what the Judge cannot formulate in words. The photograph is thus a materialization but in the form of a trace of something that cannot be seen in court. It is matterphorical in the alternate sense that it matters to the decision and provides a material presence of the structure, albeit as a trace, in the forum. Second, in being a photograph of something other than the view of the house from the rear, the aspect that is covered by the restrictive covenant in the interpretation adopted by the court, the picture repeats the essential invisibility of the ultimate source of decision while representing a trace of the structure that is the object and projection of the judgment.

The story of the storeys is multiply pertinent. Dogma is apodictic, meaning that whether in the form of a maxim, a custom inherited from time immemorial, or an image and similitude, it is a given and is not to be challenged. There is a point where reason runs out and, as the early lawyers were wont to say, authority is more important than truth. This is because the sovereign or Judge, as the case may be, has to see what

---

32 Pierre Legendre, *God in the Mirror: A Study of the Institution of Images* (London: Routledge, 2019) at 79. The sources return to Bonaventura, *De Potentia* 1.9 art. 9 c; through Thomas Aquinas, *Summa Theologica* Ia q. 4 a. 3; q. 45 a. 7; q. 93 a. 2, 6.

is not there and can only represent this in the form of image and faith. The closest we can come to the ground of a decision is that aspect of the earth that appears in the judgment, the image as the vision of the source and invention of determination. It takes us closer, as near as it is possible to get to the visceral, incarnadine source of decision. The picture of the storeys is the start of the story, the narrative, metonymically conveyed through the photograph, of the judgment. Vision generates decision and the novelty of technologies that now facilitate inserting images into precedent judgments allows for a much more direct and material analysis of the role of these visual fictions, of the unaccompanied view, of photograph, or emoji, meme, gif, and other instagrams, in the triggering of legal reason.

The building is a structure and has a façade, a face, that can be photographed. This provides a sense of the real and a mask for the Judge to wear. What can be seen hides what is unseen and so allows for the staging of the drama of the case, which is itself about vision and the ability to see over buildings but not being able to see though them. The element of staging is the key to apprehending the significance of the advent of pictures in judgments. It indicates the series of performative moments of enactment that the law engages. The Judge goes to take a photograph and to perambulate in the neighbourhood, amongst the buildings, to get a sense and to relay a sensibility. The Judge steps out of his office, enters the world, returns with it, *in imagine*, to the court. The image is proof of having seen, of having faced the abyss of the real and covered the infinite regress of origin with a trace of what was seen. The depiction is in this sense a skin, an integument that closes off any further discussion because 'here it is', the house, the issue, although of course it isn't there, merely the trace, the covering of what cannot be seen. To borrow from Ovid and the myth of Narcissus, 'he thinks he sees a body, which is but a shadow' and yet while this trace lacks substance, it nonetheless inflames and is the object of desire.[33] The image introduces affect both in that it identifies through vision and it projects the viewer spectrally into the viewed. The depiction, flat, prosaic, cluttered, ordinary nonetheless excites the senses and triggers the desire of both seeing and being seen in the Judge and in the viewer of the judgment. The image is the coda of decision, the identifiable and transferential point of judgment in which we are drawn to see what the Judge saw and attach to the principle, the visual axiom and depicted dogma that founds the reasoning that supports the decision.

---

33 Ovid, *Metamorphoses* Bk 111 at 417–19.

The image, as Ovid also points out, is always more than it seems or appears to be. This, in more contemporary terms, is because the image is apprehended distinctly and viewed differently. It is not text, and indeed from the perspective of reading, the words float in the space of the image because what is seen is subject to spectral modes of viewing. The ambulation of the eye in looking is non-linear, it wanders, traverses, darts in and out, laterally, changing focus, scotomizing, registering, glancing, thinking in its own figurative form. The principle of looking is in many respects sciographic, a dance of shadows, a play of concentration and relaxation, a lateral flitting across surfaces. Retinal justice, the equity of the eye introduces a distinct and different avenue of apprehension and analysis into the juridical text. It draws upon a separate archive of images and relays a visual trajectory and imaginal sense of the subjects of doctrine and dispute. Where previously the doctrine of precedent distinguished *ratio decidendi* and *obiter dictum*, the binding rule of judgment from the observations made along the way, the novel transition to imagery suggests that accompanying and in some cases determining the textual distinction is that between the *imago decidendi* and *obiter depicta*, the vision of decision and things seen along the way.[34] Here the apparatus of decision operates in a necessarily aesthetic and imaginative ocular form because the introduction of pictures introduces sense and sensibility into the epistemic paradigm and narrative form of the juridical text. Poetic justice is subtended by the retinal apprehension of subject matter, and by the affect and imagination of seeing, accompanied as it is by colour, where clips and links are inserted, by sound and motion as well. These are not incidental nor are they irrelevant either to the legal value of the precedent or to the allure and attachment that the text can promote in persuasion.

From the perspective of jurisliterature and the expanded humanistic tradition that the new media both allow and promote, the propaedeutic purposes, potential and accessibility of the juristic text are greatly expanded. The sensibility of the depiction brings with it an array of affective and unconscious links, images, and connotations. The division of discourse and figure, word and image borrows, of course, from Freud's *The Interpretation of Dreams* and specifically his elaboration

---

[34] For expansion of these themes, see Goodrich, 'Pictures as Precedents: The Visual Turn and the Status of Figures in Judgments', in Anker and Meyler (eds), *New Directions in Law and Literature* (Oxford: Oxford University Press, 2017) at 176; and further Goodrich, 'Retinal Justice: Rats, Maps and Masks' (2021) 47 *Critical Inquiry* 241.

of the image as the medium of dream work to elicit the two principal axes of interpretation, those of condensation and displacement. Condensation refers to the compression of the dream and thus to the enigmatic and layered quality of the figure as the singular representation or point of intersection of several associative chains. As a nodal point, the condensation is also marked by intensity of energy and excess of meaning, which is itself the result of displacement. The latter term refers to the decentring characteristic of the dream. It draws the analyst's attention to the latent content of the dream, which exists in a lateral and otherwise focused relation to its manifest content. As Lyotard translates this, 'The position of art is a refutation of the position of discourse ... Art stands in alterity as plasticity and desire, a curved expanse against invariability and reason, diacritical space.'[35] The image brings to the surface of the jurist's expression what was hitherto hidden by the linearity of the word and the juridical conception of reason as free of passion. Appearance here becomes the spatial signal and symptom of depth: 'One only has to allow oneself to slip into the well of discourse to find the eye lodged at its core ... The figure is both without and within.' To this one might add the medieval poetic and philosophical maxim *ubi amor, ibi oculos* – where the eye is, there is love.

The figure and now the pictorial depiction in the precedent is thus to be understood as that which drives judgment and makes – figures – the decision. The theatrical and performative exercises of legal reason become suddenly visible and so at the same time contestable in a more transparent and potentially egalitarian frame. Take the example of a US Judge who is most fond, an advocate and a leader in the field of judicial use of images in judgments. The uses that judges make of imagery may not as yet be particularly sophisticated nor critically self-conscious of the epistemic and ontological questions raised but they are exposing. Despite explicitly advocating for images in precedents, Posner exhibits a certain blindness to the differential status of the scenes depicted and proceeds largely in ignorance of the anachronic or at least trans-temporal relay of imagery that comes along with, and that is carried as undertow or rhizomatic archive in every image.[36]

---

35 Jean-François Lyotard, *Discourse, Figure* [1971] (Minnesota: University of Minneapolis Press, 2011) at 7.
36 Posner's argument is made most explicitly in Richard Posner, 'Judicial Opinions and Appellate Advocacy in Federal Courts – One Judge's Views' (2013) 51 *Duquesne L. Rev.* 3, at 12–13. For a brief judicial instance of that argument made visually, see *Gonzalez-Servin v. Ford Motor Co.*, 662

What he does do, in unison now with a growing number of judges throughout the common law world, is insert a diversity of pictures and hyperlinks into the reasoning of decisions and it is this precedential impact that requires attention. The initial point is that the image is never singular, its plurality implying the interconnectivity of iconic and familiar within the screen and framing of any depiction. This needs to be recognized and worked on at many levels of epistemic and affective impact, as can be gleaned from another cautionary instance. In *Sikhs for Justice v Badal*, the plaintiffs sought to serve an injunction upon the defendant (*in absentia*), the Chief Minister of Punjab, under the Alien Torts Statute, for extrajudicial killings and torture, in violation of customary international law and the Torture Victim Protection Act of 1991, committed by the Punjab police while he was responsible for overseeing all security services. The Judge expresses a certain enthusiasm for the case, a touch of exuberance appearing in his definition of the issue: 'This appeal presents a single issue, which is whether the defendant was served with process; yet the case could be the basis for a novel of international intrigue.'[37]

Judge Posner's remark about the novel should not be viewed as innocent. He is also a lecturer in law, the author of a study of *Law and Literature* as a misunderstood relation, and of many essays on Shakespeare and other literary figures. He recognizes even in the first edition of the book that the study of law 'is undergoing fundamental change' but his thesis is primarily that law and literature is an academic exercise and of marginal practical value, whatever soul enhancing effects it may have on lawyers and critics.[38] The dismissal of fundamental change to the cloistered realm of scholarly elaborations and pedagogic pursuits leads both to undermining the fundamental character of the change, and to ignoring the novelistic character of his own development of the facts of the case. The reference to the novel is symptomatic of the fiction that he is engaged in developing. In the Judge's own account, the plaintiffs hired a process server, Christopher Kratochvil, and showed him a video and gave him a picture of Badal: 'The photograph and the video showed a tall, thin, elderly man with a long white beard and a mustache, wearing a turban (mandatory for

---

F.3d 931 (7th Cir. 2011); discussed at length in Goodrich, Imago decidendi: *The Common Law of Images* (Leiden: Brill, 2017).

37 *Sikhs for Justice v Badal* 736 F.3d 743 (2013).
38 Richard Posner, *Law and Literature: A Misunderstood Relation* (Cambridge, MA: Harvard University Press, 1988) at 362.

Sikh men) and eyeglasses' and instructed him to serve the defendant during a ceremony at a High School in Milwaukee that the defendant was due to attend. (Figure 4.4) The process server claimed to have duly served Badal, but the defense argued that he had served another Sikh, a teacher named Kalra. The Judge reproduces a photograph of Badal and one of Kalra (Figure 4.5) and proceeds to elucidate upon the fictive import of the images.

Of the images, the Judge states that they support the trial court's determination: 'What makes the judge's finding especially convincing is Kalra's resemblance to the defendant, as seen in the photographs in the appendix to this opinion.'[39] We tend to look 'unconsciously' at the outer features of a face, hairstyle and 'one imagines a turban, rather than giving equal weight to everything we see in the face'.[40] To this, the Judge adds the flourish that 'people of one race sometimes have difficulty perceiving facial differences in people of a different race'.[41] Such would certainly seem to be the case with the Judge himself. The point is not that the two parties look strikingly different, nor that the photographs reproduced are in such poor monochrome quality as to conceal as much as they reveal, but rather that the Judge is defining the images reproduced by reading texts into them, asserting in effect: we do not generally recognize difference, we look at clothes, facial attire, rather than the face, as race generates unfamiliarity and triggers non-recognition. That may be true of the protected social circles and homogeneous peer group in which the Judge mixes, but it is an extraordinary projection on to a process server whose job and métier is that of recognizing individuals in all clothes, colours, guises and disguises. Discrimination in vision means looking more closely, but this is precisely what the Judge fails to do,

Figure 4.4 *Sikhs for Justice v Badal – case files*

---

39 *Sikhs for Justice* at 744.
40 Ibid., at 747.
41 Ibid.

Figure 4.5 *Sikhs for Justice v Badal – case files*

remaining on the exterior even of the visage, looking at costume and follicles rather than at the *imago* or face itself.

The Judge uses the pictures to tell a story:

> Kratochvil is not an Indian, and not a Sikh. To the non-Sikh the salient features of a Sikh man are abundant facial hair and a turban. If the man is elderly, the beard will be white. The photo that Kratochvil was carrying to enable him to spot the defendant showed an elderly man with a long white beard and a turban. Kratochvil had been told that the man in the photo would be at the high school, presumably in a place of prominence since the defendant is a very prominent Sikh (even if hated by the SFJ) – and bingo, at the head of the room Kratochvil sees a man who closely resembles the man in the photo . . . So Kratochvil makes a beeline for him, hands him the papers and flees before the man has a chance to ask him what is this all about and to tell him that by the way his name is not Badal.

The images trigger a narrative that would likely not otherwise have emerged in the judgment, evidencing the drive of decision and the latent content of the pictures in the novelistic fiction that the Judge uses to describe the imaginal scene of process delivery. The photographs condense affect relating to race, allowing the Judge to discourse on facial hair and turbans, beards and colour, similarity and difference of race and identity. The images allow an unguarded glimpse of the judicial imagination because the photographs are there, everyone can see them and in the mind of the Judge they show what he perceives, a unity, identities without significant differentiation – in the Augustinian analysis so foundational for the West – *imago simillima rei* – an image that is in all aspects similar to the thing seen. The juridical viewer, however, is the agent of the unification, and in the mode of projection attributes to the other what he misrecognizes in himself, treating the inability to differentiate Sikh individuals as a feature of the external world. The Judge places the stamp of cultural identity on the other, viewed through the lens of white perception and the narrative of our identity compared to their difference. The desire to be seen is the same as the desire that triggers seeing. The Judge in essence sees himself as the proper affect and vision of the world, projecting his perception on to that of the participants in the dispute. That the image is the dogma, means that the picture seen, the reflection of Narcissus in the water, is the structuring principle of vision, the desire for the self in the other.

It might seem that the occasional insertion of images into judgments is of little direct significance to the interpretation of the narratives and other fictions of law. It could also be argued that images are already the subject of extensive forensic rhetorical analysis, the figures of speech being the means by which the orator renders reason vivid (*vividæ rationes*) and brings the actions described before the eyes of the auditor. There is considerable truth in such claims and the curricular tradition offers much by way of analysis of the visual character of the affective dimensions of legal discourse, as also of the symptoms and slips of expression. Legal imagination flowers in many forms but what the novel technologies of pictorial representation introduce is a foundational level of invention and a visualization of the affect that drives thought. This is the imaginal dimension of legality, in which, as noted before, the imaginal references a space of suspended ontology, of the image as extant between the real and the imaginary. The imaginal has been analysed here as trace and screen of the vanishing point where law encounters what it cannot formulate and does not know. Like Narcissus, Judge Posner sees what he does not know and covers it with a photograph so as to provide the appearance of knowledge of the invisible, the real, which in this case is the identity of Sikhs at an event where a process was served.

The judicial recourse to photographs indicates in the most direct available manner the motive and the imagination, the vision that underpins decision. It is what theologians term the aereall sign, the vanishing signifier of the origin. The imaginal is the closest it is possible to get to what is not there, the non-present whose trace alone remains. The image is here the last haptic point, the moment of dematerialization, in which vision dissipates into reality, otherwise defined as the unknown. The logic of disappearance constitutes, in the image, the last instance of the visible and so the staging of what has to be represented. Manifestation of what is not present is precisely the didactic and theatrical principle of the jurisliterary which endeavours to manifest, elegantly, aesthetically, materially, the imagination that as law will hold the group together. To do this in pictures is to activate a different modality of performativity and a distinct set of possibilities lodged at the level of desire and according to the non-analogical relations of appearances. The visual does not proceed by similarity in the sense of analogy but according to apparent connections and the rhizomatic multiplicity of visibilities, the law of the spectacle.

5 Transitions

The most extraordinary and legally misunderstood jurisliterary narrative of the modern era must surely be that of Judge Daniel Paul Schreber. Trained in the mid-nineteenth century in the style of German historical positivism, he worked on the great Civil Code, the quintessence of juristic rationalism, and then as a magistrate and latterly a Supreme Court Judge and President of one Chamber of the highest Court of Appeal. The story is well known in psychiatric and psychoanalytic literatures but not in jurisprudence or jurisliterature and hence my recapitulation of some brief details. Towards the end of the century, the epoch of the third sex, of the suffragettes and the push for political and professional emancipation of women, the Judge tired of his virile judicial role, lost faith in jurisprudence and fell sick of law. It is not so uncommon for lawyers to seek to escape, to pursue more creative passions, but Schreber is exceptional for the form that hir extra-judicial writings took – the *Memoirs* are still in print over a century later – and for the content of their indisposition, the belief that he was becoming a woman, that his body was unfolding in the feminine, that Miss Schreber was appearing in front of the mirror.[1]

The story, *in nuce* and eggshell, is that the Judge had attempted to escape law by standing for election to the Reichstag (Parliament) in the Fall of 1884 and lost. The failure, I have argued elsewhere, led to the first episode of dysphoria and transitional desire.[2] It landed Schreber in a Leipzig University clinic run by Professor Flechsig. The demand for normalcy was re-imposed but the Judge, as Mark Sanders brilliantly points out, nonetheless retained severe doubts and complains at one point that his doctors had failed to explain to him how to operate

---

1 Daniel Paul Schreber, *Memoirs of My Nervous Illness* [1903] (Cambridge, MA: Harvard University Press, 1988).

2 Peter Goodrich, *Schreber's Law: Jurisprudence and Judgment in Transition* (Edinburgh: Edinburgh University Press, 2018). See also Peter Goodrich and Katrin Trüstedt (eds), *Laws of Transgression: The Return of Judge Schreber* (Toronto: University of Toronto Press, 2021).

the scales at the clinic and so impeded his ability to weigh himself.[3] Unable to judge his own weight, without proper balance, Schreber could hardly be surprised if later he was ill equipped to apply equitable measure and proper proportion to legal disputes. Returning to work and eight years later being appointed to the Presidency of the Royal Court in Dresden, the malaise of law returned in force and a second break out attempt ensued. This time *morbus juridicus* is more severe and Schreber explicitly abandons the virile profession of law in favour of pursuing his own transition: 'I have wholeheartedly inscribed the cultivation of femininity on my banner, and I will continue to do so as far as consideration of my environment allows. . . .' And after that vexillological declaration of independence and of cause, the Judge continues to advert to the most obvious consequence, the transformative impact of such a transitional motif upon his erstwhile institutional roles:

> The pursuit of my previous profession, which I loved wholeheartedly, every other aim of manly ambition, and every other use of my intellectual powers in the service of mankind, are now all closed to me through the way circumstances have developed; even communication with my wife . . .[4]

Both *oikonomic* and administrative roles are precluded, foreclosed by the transition, the Judge claiming, performing, inventing a new body and a different world.

In the 1890s, in Saxony, the President of the Royal Court of Appeals third chamber declares that they are stepping down to become a woman and to reform the Order of the World (*Weltordnung*) which is perilously out of joint. It is a project that is theological, philosophical and scientific and in Schreber's persistently argued view will be proven both physically and theoretically true. His body is offered to science, while he also maintains consistently that they are not and have never been mad although often in the circumstances surrounded by lunatics. Transition not the failure of reason is the cause of their difference. There will be pain, there will be costs and consequences, and not least for that reason the mutating jurist will keep a meticulous record of their experiences that ultimately lead to the successful conclusion of

---
3 Mark Sanders, 'Psychoanalysis, Mourning, and the Law: Schreber's Paranoia as Crisis of Judging,' in Austin Sarat and Martha Merrill Umphrey (eds), *Law and Mourning* (Amherst: University of Massachusetts Press, 2017) at 131.
4 Schreber, *Memoirs*, at 149.

the lawsuit for release from confinement in the asylum. The Court of Appeals that adjudges him mad (*wahnhaften*) but legally competent even remarks on how his delusional ideas 'by the way are developed and motivated with remarkable clarity and logical precision'.[5] It is not here, however, the rhetorical verve or juristic language and finesse of the *Memoirs* and their accompanying performances in court that are at issue, save to give a sense of the hostility of the environment and the crashing moral and psychiatric law of sexual normalcy that Schreber faced. The radical novelty of the work lies rather in its ontography, the novel epistemic that the transitional jurist espouses and expresses through body writing, through corporeal sensibility, through a theory of knowing as a physical phenomenon, a drama of the flesh.

It starts in the Fall of 1884. He starts hearing noises in the walls, he pays attention to his phantasies – his hypnopompic vision that 'it must be rather beautiful to be a woman succumbing (*unterliege*) to intercourse', and senses change in body and soul.[6] The body is already, in this first phase, the focus of dysphoria and symptoms of weight loss, and sleeplessness, the inability to weigh himself, incomprehension of what his senses are telling himher are its expression. With the second symbolic collapse, the so called 'investiture crisis' – although aren't they all? – the epistemic drive is to know the body, to prove corporeal change, to challenge philosophy and science with the corporeal sensibilities of a transitional subject. The narrative of proof may seem overly juristic, and the language frequently is for necessary reasons, but the point is that it is corporeal sense that provides the insights: 'When the rays approach, my breast gives the impression of a pretty well-developed female bosom; this phenomenon can be seen by anybody who wants to observe me with his own eyes. I am therefore in a position to offer objective evidence by observation of my body.'[7] The disquisitions on corporeal change, the unfolding of desire through the tensors and nerves of the body gain multiple expressions throughout the work. The genitals contract, breasts are formed, the torso slims, the buttocks and legs become feminine, and at various poignant and playful junctures she points to the telos of the process:

---

5 *Memoirs*, at 273. This point is taken up with élan by Katrin Trüstedt, 'Schreber's Double Process: Legal and Literary transformations in the *Memoirs of my Nervous Illness*', in Goodrich and Trüstedt (eds), *Schreber's Transition* (Toronto: Toronto University Press, 2021).

6 Ibid., 63.

7 Ibid., 207.

the signs of transformation into a woman became so marked on my body, that I could no longer ignore the imminent goal at which the whole development was aiming ... Soul-voluptuousness had become so strong that I myself received the impression of a female body, first on my arms and hands, later on my legs, bosom, buttocks and other parts of my body.[8]

Finally, disruptively, erotically, a Judge who recognizes the folds and tensions of the skin, the desires of the flesh, the mobility and transitivity of bodily performances and the role of the senses in cognition.

Schreber, dysphoric, sick of law, confused and in pain strives for difference. The end of the process is a mixed sexuality, a fluid and constantly shifting combination of organs, extremities, looks, sounds and perceptions. The body mutates when the Judge thinks of it, the breasts swell and contract, the buttocks morph, limbs shift from thick to thin. Female accessories, the 'armamentarium' of clothing, the mirror phase of gender change all combine to create a new mode of knowing the body and a novel apprehension and knowledge of the world. This is not for Schreber alone. Anticipating over a century of future gender troubles, the Judge increasingly understands both the choice of gender and sex, as well as the performative character of transitional identity. It is not just Miss Schreber pleasingly reflected in the mirror. It is also a question of attire, appearances and apparel creating a momentary image and performance of a mutable identity. An impersonality is being chosen and this is a question both of being in the world, a matter of the appearance created, and of the internal sensibility that can project and repeat it so that 'the rays [get the] impression that my body has female breasts and a female sexual organ'.[9] Thus the Judge can engage, know and challenge externality, variously depicted in terms of rays, nerves, automata, writing down machines, fleeting improvised beings, miracles, noises, voices, higher and lower gods.

The primary mode in which Schreber enters the confused and out of joint Order of the World, is through a corporeal sensibility that struggles constantly against the condemnation of the doctors and the dismissal of the lawyers and it is against that hostility that an implicit theory of law develops. It starts with the imaginal, a mode of apprehending and influencing through what is termed picturing. Mentioned in the same passage as the description of standing in front of the

---

8 Ibid., 148.
9 Ibid., 181.

mirror, the ability to picture is defined as 'a reverse miracle', in effect an attempt to counter the political theology of the established Order of the World with independence of thought and changeable gender performances. Picturing is variously depicted as visions, as more than words, as imagination that enters the world and in conjunction with the rays, the divine lines of light and sense, creates the spectral dominion of nature. The world for Schreber is one of visceral and vivid sensory impressions absorbed by the nerves and rays as pictures that are stored in the nervous system: 'To picture (in the sense of the soul-language) is the conscious use of the human imagination for the purpose of producing pictures (predominantly pictures of recollection) in one's head which can be looked at by rays . . . these images become visible either inside my head or if I wish, outside'. Pictures bring change and joy, allowing the Judge at one point to be in different places, playing the piano and 'standing in front of the mirror in an adjoining room in female attire'.[10] The imaginal is calming and curative, the harmony of musical composition allowing Miss Schreber the pleasure of identifying, in part, in front of the mirror as a different *ens non imaginaria*, a distinctive 'as if' of performativity.[11] To picture is to project in a cinematic sense, to give shape to things, and to people, to miraculous phenomena including the change on Schreber's own person '*which probably will become more and more marked in the future* and will lead other human beings of necessity to recognize their truth'.[12] What is pictured is proleptically real, it will become and be accepted in the future and this is peculiarly true of Schreber's experience. Life becomes art, and art enters life. The painting in their head becomes the image in the world.

The high office holder who stepped down, the demitted Judge, the asylum inmate creates a universe of connectivity in which the nerves in their body extended outwards into the world as the world in turn enters their body. Through music and picturing, in an aesthetic mode, the *Memoirs* conjure an imaginal imperson, a plural array of corporeal performances and gender attributes that enter and fight to change the world. It is a remarkable, critical and deeply self-reflexive autobiographical narrative of pain and miracle, body and soul strug-

---

10 Ibid., 180–181.
11 For purposes of research and as itself a finely 'as if' enterprise, see Hans Vaihinger, *The Philosophy of 'As If. A System of the Theoretical, Practical and Religious Fictions of Mankind* (Trans. C.K. Ogden; London: Kegan Paul, 1924).
12 *Memoirs*, at 186.

gling for expression, undergoing – succumbing – to transformation, reconfiguration, different décor and dress, appearance and apparel. It is also unique in jurisliterature. It provides the only existential account of a *corpus iuris*, a judicial body in transition and escape from the iron cage of high Judicial office. The *Memoirs* provide a visceral picture of the madness of law. They open the doors of legal reason to provide a glimpse of the desire and the folly that also inhabit the temple of justice, stalk the interior corridors and disrupt the cerebra of legality.

In the argute argot of contemporary trans discourses, Schreber is still, over a century since his death, at the forefront of the most radical attack upon juridical theology and specifically upon the binary distinction, and opposition, the inapposite biblical choice – *masculum et foeminam fecit eos* – between male and female.[13] The Judge flitted between the roles and the bodies of prior sexual designation, and in the process abandoned the abstraction of legal doctrine for the immediacy and sensory plenitude of matter, the body and in the jargon of the *Memoirs*, the nerves and rays. Schreber stepped out of his office so as to fight the symbolic law of sexual division and the juridical methods and constraints that kept it so separated. Here one could say is a jurisliterary introduction to legality, a critical didactic work that both shows how law works – the lawsuit for release from the asylum was successful – and how irrelevant the architectonic and exclusively linguistic theories and pure jurisprudences are to the sensibilities, the operations and attributions of everyday experience, the dominions of chance, encounter, matter and desire. The Judge sought to enter the miraculous and voluptuous order of hir own desire, their law, unconstrained by either purity or the exclusivity of abstraction.

What better introduction to the complexities and conflicts of law than a work by an inside outsider, an ex-Judge, a transitional jurist – recollect that Schreber continued to act as a lawyer after being adjudged legally competent and released from the asylum – who confronts the eager young, desiring youth, with the desideratum that they choose their variable gender roles, that they think through their bodies, that they apprehend legality in a more sophisticated and connected mode than mere abstraction and rules. Gods, sovereigns, oligarchs, autocrats and ochlocrats are impugned as obstacles to self-definition and freedom of

---

13 For one instance of direct attack upon the requirement of choice, see Paul B. Preciado, *Testo Junkie: Sex, Drugs, and Biopolitics in the Pharmacopornographic Era* (New York: Feminist Press, 2016).

choice. The *Memoirs*, however, are much more than a simple epistemological challenge to a conventional, essentially Christian, neo-Kantian jurisprudence. The ontography that Schreber practices is of radical heuristic import, comprising at root an attack on the hermeneutic institution of legalism and its exclusion of diversity of thought and feeling. The most obvious object of critique is God and the hierarchies of law and sex. The Gods, higher and lower, Ariman and Ozmud, are noisy, extraneous, irrelevant and ill-informed about tellurian existence, train schedules, and human needs. The dominion of divinities is death, and as Spinoza remarks, life is for the living, and the world should be free of the interferences and disturbances of extra-terrestrial, incorporeal, imaginary anthropomorphic beings. It is *tellus*, earth, Gaia that should govern and in whose spirit the rays and the nerves connect all beings and collectively confabulate the community of thought.

Schreber's strictures are directed next toward the automata, the writing down machines that simply inscribe everything and through the rays endeavour to fill the subject's head with the noise of abstraction and the repetition of meaningless phrases and broken off sentences. The writing down system is expressive of compulsive thinking and is a system of 'falsifying thought'.[14] The key characteristic of this automaton scriptorium is incomprehensibility to humans, and frequently meaningless repetition of unconnected phrases, as well as a prolixity that verges on encompassing all of human language. The writing down system is attributed to fleeting improvised beings, sketchy, spectral entities, in a word lawyers and particularly the images of those wardens, guardians, court officials, procurators and prosecutors who had so vigorously sought to confine and exclude the Judge.[15] The writing down and questioning of Schreber is law as 'play-with-human-beings' and is tied to celestial bodies, to abstraction, and to the continuous attempt to govern their thoughts and emotions through a relentless onslaught of dissipated phrases. Law and lawyers are distractions from the Judge's proper cause which is to sculpt and body and build a world fit for strawberries, a community of the senses, an aesthetic legality undaunted by desire, *elegantior iuris* being taken here in the etymological sense of *elegans* whose primary meaning in Lewis and Short is effeminate. That sense should be included.

---

14 *Memoirs*, at 70.
15 Ibid., 235–6.

As a heuristic, the Judge's method is that of opening the body to the nerves and rays, to sensation and world. They, the plurality of the person, vociferate and bellow, play music, have visions, write, record and register for their own purposes, which are principally those of inscribing corporeal and other sensory changes as significant and worthy of thought. These are what Gandorfer depicts as thoughts worthy of thinking, a high bar, a different bar, an alternate future profession that has yet to be defined outside of divine interventions and compulsory modes of predetermined thought.[16] Thinking in and with the body, posing the endless question:

> How to think critically without falling into the habits of universalizing, generalizing, analogizing, and, consequently, erasing bodies and embodiments in law? Indeed, how to prevent a future that threatens to seamlessly connect to a past that has already reached its verdict over what law *is*?[17]

How then, as Schreber also depicts it, to avoid the stultifying laws of thought that pre-empt the sensorium and anarchy of transitional and transformative thinking? How can thought be forged to matter? The thinking subject needs to be able to choose the time and space of their thinking and, equally important for the Judge, challenge and rebuff non-thinking, 'the not-thinking-of-anything-thought', the ceaseless chatter of the voices and the 'senseless monotony like a barrel-organ [of] all the other tasteless forms of speech'.[18] Escape from the strain of compulsive thinking, the script of automata, the pull of the past and of conventional dictation requires asserting that thought matters.

The humanist and now trans-humanist jurisliterary enterprise of introducing and expatiating the culture, habitus and ethos of law is one which paints law amongst the other disciplines and expounds the theatrical and affective dimensions of legal rule. The older language spoke, as discussed earlier, of *artes quae vitam instruant*, of another poetry (*alius poeta*) and comparable vision of social life as an affair of

---

16 Gandorfer, 'Embodied Critique and Posthuman(ist) Legal Futures. Things Worth More than Being Thought. Judge Schreber. Madness. Think!' in *Laws of Transgression*, 'Schreber's head hurts, but he is far from surrendering – he has big thoughts, *denkwürdig* (worthy to be thought). Somewhere in his process, oscillating between speculative investigation and meticulous self-examination, unable to find sane answers to mad questions, Schreber takes a decision: in order to help his fellow human beings overcome a law that doesn't do bodies well, he has to write his patient and case history, his memoirs, *Denkwürdigkeiten*, things worth thinking . . .'
17 Gandorfer, 'Things Worth More than Being Thought', at 32.
18 *Memoirs*, at 154.

eros and amity, of the friendship of disciplines – *circulus disciplinarum* – and of the community of thought whose structures are necessarily poetic and juridical. The *Memoirs* take this focus and vision further in dramatic ways by extending focus from ornament to actuality, from costume to corporeality, from abstraction to action. Schreber also introduces vision, the picturing of connection, and the erotic tensors of knowledge as material expression, inclusive of bellowing, apparitions, speaking birds, the exothermic allotropes of nature, and the aporia of others. The question posed is that of what matters, towards whom desire is to be directed, which causes attract and drive the jurist and the community to which they belong. *Elegans jurisprudentia* is a gender mixed enterprise and begins for Schreber with the body as a mobile and mutating form of sense and desire, apprehension and hapticity that generates thoughts worth thinking.

The transitional vision of altered connections promulgates a different conception of community and an augmented sense of intellective commonality. The amity of law is expanded and the erotic and erogenous facets of thought are installed finally in the body that thinks and the intellection that ensues. Where matterphorical theory challenges abstraction on the basis that thinking is always also embodied, affective, and mobile, new materialism insists upon the performance that renders judgment in all instances of expression and not least in legal determinations. The theory of performance as kinesthetic and connected, as transitional and relational propagates a new mode of thinking law as a mode of apprehension and imbrication in the world. What matters is relational and affective, our amity for community and ideas, our links to others, to other species and the organism of the earth (*humus*), the transhuman and the transhumusian. Schreber and Gandorfer agree that machines lack bodies and affect and therefore cannot think organically but only in digital binaries or as automata. There is a bigger picture that it is the function of the jurisliterary to introduce and promulgate. As Forcadel puts it in *Cupid's Jurisprudence*, fiction and poetry, a necessary aesthetic, form the foundation of law and constitute its most intimate recess and resource.[19] The springs of action and the triggers of invention are the exigency of legal poetics and both connect the juridical to its practices and paint the bigger picture of equity and justice as the parameters and limits of legal performance.

---

19 Stephanus Forcatulus, *Cupido iurisperitus* (1553) – *iura sanctissima fabulis et carminibus permiscere*.

It was, recollect, for Schreber, being adorned in feminine accoutrements and accessories, in the armamentarium of female dress, that a curative practice, a healing imaginal motion occurred. Looking in the mirror and seeing Miss Schreber, the body and costume of a feminine side to the Schreberian self, allowed a shift, a transition in atmosphere and a mutation of the self. I, as the erstwhile Judge would have it, am another, and the sensibility of that plurality is carried by costume. As the philosopher Coccia formulates it, our sensible life is manifested in our image, the external materialization of our perception of self. It is in full consonance with Schreber's transitional practices, that he elaborates:

> Nature lives first and foremost as dress [*veste*]. Or better, it is foremost in dress, in our becoming image, that we first discover the possibility of existing outside and beyond ourselves . . . In the sensible life, we can be born and rise again continuously, without ever presupposing a past or a history, and without needing to transform ourselves. We are eternal thanks only to fashion, only to the degree in which we are able to transform our most profound nature into dress (acquirable by all) and, vice versa, transform the fashion from which we live into our nature. True eternity is not immortality; it is not what awaits us after death. Nor is it what resists our destruction. Rather, it is what is transferable and appropriable by all. Only the sensible is truly eternal; only the image is truly eternal. Fashion is the organ of this eternity.[20]

Schreber uses dress to identify gender and transition. It is clothes that make up the image of the person and the person of the image. It is a very simple and long-recognized humanist principle that we are what we inherit and what we make of it. What matters is matter, the textiles and the texts that attract, the communities we join, the circles of disciplines and fashions to which we belong. These are our friends, our companion textiles and texts, our intellective fellow travellers, the appearances and words, costumes and customs in which we bathe, the tensors and tactile temptations of the everyday.[21] Might the *actus reus*, phonetically ray us, be the art of getting dressed? No matter, much matter, we are never immune to spatial configurations, apparel

---

20 Emanuele Coccia, *Sensible Life: A Micro-ontology of the Image* (New York: Fordham University Press, 2015) at 96.
21 An argument well made in Gary Watt, 'Dress, Law and the Naked Truth: Some Further Coverage' (2016) 7 *Critical Studies in Fashion & Beauty* 109, at 118: 'Dress is order, and in a culture where the order of dress takes the form of clothes, public nudity may be perceived as an assault upon the very core of the civilizing project.'

and appearance, aspect and image, though we often deny. *Felix ars iuris*, the performance of justice, is as much as anything else a question of recognition of our intellective friendships and our sentiments of belonging and hence of what is properly artistic and necessary for justice. A simple example or two will suffice and satisfy. In *Textile Unlimited v A..BMH and Co.*, a Californian contracts case, the issue was that of whether the defendants could be enjoined to arbitration in Georgia, the domicile of A..BMH and Co.[22] This question turned on the terms of the contract and the thread that tied the parties to each other over a plurality of transactions. Textile had ordered wool from the Georgia supplier on 37 occasions over the prior year. On each occasion Textile would fill out a purchase order form, specifying the item number, quantity and price. A..BMH would then respond with an invoice, shipment and order acknowledgment. A..BMH's paper purported to make the contract conditional upon acceptance of their terms, which included mandatory arbitration in Georgia and governed by Georgia law. On each occasion, Textile took shipment and paid but refused to pay for the 38th shipment on the ground that the wool was defective. It is a complicated doctrinal issue, differently determined in different US jurisdictions, as to how the notoriously poorly drafted section 2:207 of the Uniform Commercial Code applies to repeat transactions such as these. That, however, is not really the big picture, which is whether the purchaser had agreed to the terms. Show me the facts and I will show you the law, as the maxim goes.

Sitting in Pasadena, California, Judge Thomas of the ninth circuit United States Court of Appeals opens by formulating the dispute: 'Textile Unlimited, Inc. . . . claims that A..BMH is, in the parlance of the industry, spinning a yarn . . . A..BMH counters that Textile is warping the facts.' Then to the action: 'Over the course of ten months of this tangled affair Textile bought goods from A..BMH in approximately thirty-eight transactions. Each followed a similar pattern.' That particular transactional weave is depicted as an invoice and order acknowledgement that 'contained a twist . . . additional terms tucked into the back of the invoice and the face of the acknowledgment, terms that had not adorned Textile's purchase order . . .' Textile does not request 'any alterations' but argues that the arbitration clause had not been 'woven into the contract'. And then, 'with arbitration looming', Textile files an action to enjoin the arbitration commenced by A..BMH in Georgia. 'Unruffled' the Arbitrator moved forward. Judge Thomas

---

22 *Textile Unlimited v A..BMH* 240 F.3d 781 (2001).

then traces 'the threads' of the relevant Federal jurisprudence and finds the 'narrowly tailored' rules governing venue to favour Textile. At first glance the metaphoricity of the judgment seems not to matter. It is doctrinally merely ornamental, a jurisliterary incident, an exornation to the logic of the statute and the jurisprudence of decision. Think again. The interweaving of woollen metaphors is in the strictest of senses matterphorical and entirely apposite. It may seem to be a joke, but in jurisliterary vision it is a matter of *in ludo veritas*, the puns contain an important and implicitly transitional truth.

The subject matter of the numerous transactions is textile, from the Latin *textilis*, meaning a web, canvas, woven fabric, or cloth. The most directly pertinent question before the court was whether the web of transactions or canvas of contractual exchanges had woven the disputed terms into the agreements or had they been hidden in the cloth paper or text of the bargain? Text, from the Latin *textus*, shares a common Indo-European root with *textilis*, and both derive from things woven and threaded together. Contract, for Cicero, is amity. Historically the good faith of mutual obligation, the *consensus ad idem*, is synonymous with kinship as friendship in that both are questions of patterns of proximity, of close connection, of ties that bind. In our case that amicable connectivity is played out at two levels, that of the transaction with its textile thread, and that of the text which has to weave the subject matter into the agreement. Usually, positivistically, lawyers would start with the latter, the abstract remonstrances of the text, the airy verbiage of contract terms. What is signal and significant in the *allegoresis* of the judgment is that it starts, admittedly elliptically, with the question of textile, the weaving, warping and woofing, of wool. Another body, a non-human, woollen matter generates the drive of the judgment, the vision of decision. The complaint is that the textile is not properly woven, the threads are defective – 'not of merchantable quality' – and they are being jettisoned on that knotty basis. In parallel and consequence, the text, like the textile is also rejected for being improperly threaded. Many courts take the position of 'business practicality' and take the view that if documents have been received 38 times without objection, the recipient can be taken to be aware of them and by implication to have accepted them. Judge Thomas is cut from different cloth and takes a broader approach. There is an aura of bad faith or trickery in terms that are prolix, convoluted, imperialistic and protested too much. They have not been knit into the fabric nor agreed by the recipient. The cut is incomplete.

The striking feature of the judgment is the punning use of figures of weaving to assess the text. The pun may seem incidental but it is the rhetorical device by which we challenge the complacency of meaning and unsettle the prejudices or prior judgments brought to the text. Here the surprise arises out of the Judge beginning with matter and so approaching the text from the textile. Performance precedes the writing, because what is not well woven cannot be felicitously written. The law comes alive because it is generated by and connected to the woollen bodies, the threaded matter, the defrocked cloth bought and sold. Borrowing from Leiboff's *Theatrical Jurisprudence*, the precedent has spilled over into life and like poor theatre or post dramatic staging, the judgement has embodied the textile subject matter that lies at the root of the dispute. The text wove a well woofed new textile to replace the damaged cloth. The Judge is saved by his madness, an 'awareness beyond the self', the genius of sense which has allowed him to notice the fabric of the dispute and to become aware of and respond to, rather than merely 'verballing' the subject matter in contention.[23] The wool has been taken from law's eyes, the Judge notices, responds, enters the world, renders justice according to the interior recesses of the transacted exchange.

It is noticing, attending to the body, performing appropriately, catching the smile that forms on the lips of the auditor in response to the warp of the facts that constitute in visceral fashion the vivid and vital features of poetic justice. Judge Thomas provides an early version of wild jurisprudence in which the law is approached from a non-human perspective, the material in dispute providing the frame and the trigger of decision. As Rogers poses the wild law question: 'How do we interpret or deconstruct our existing law/laws wildly, such that humanity is not necessarily the primary focus?'[24] In *Donoghue v Stevenson* it would thus also be the interests of the snail that provide the ground of judgment and in *Textile* it is textile that marks the abyssal limit of the human.[25] Appropriately enough, with a fuller sense of justice, the connective tissue of textile prompts a more expansive connectivity and relation to earth, animal life, wool from the backs of sheep, texts,

---

23 Marett Leiboff, *Towards a Theatrical Jurisprudence* (London: Routledge, 2020) at 37.

24 Nicole Rogers, 'Performance and Pedagogy in the Wild Law Judgment Project' (2017) 27 *Legal Education Rev*. 53. For the project of Earth Jurisprudence and Wild Law Judgments, see Nicole Rogers and Michelle Maloney (eds), *Law as if Earth Really Mattered: The Wild Law Judgment Project* (London: Routledge, 2017).

25 On the snail, see Bee Chen Goh and Tom Round, 'Wild Negligence: Donoghue v Stevenson' in Rogers and Maloney (eds), *The Wild Law Judgment Project*, at 91, 106.

historically at least plea rolls, made from their skin, and mutton the main menu item in the Inns of Court. Nor does the decision stand entirely alone, unwoven or defrocked. In the English case of *Baird Textile Holdings Limited v Marks and Spencer plc*, similar issues arose and the *res gestae*, the gestures and jests of judgment take an equally proleptic and nascently pataphysical turn in the *Feminist Judgments* re-rendering of the decision.[26]

Baird is another relational case and in this instance the Plaintiff manufacturer had been working closely with the Defendant company for 30 years. The businesses had grown together in a symbiotic relationship 'akin to a partnership or subsidiary relationship' in which some 60 seasonal six-monthly contracts for specific lines of clothing had been transacted. Marks and Spencer provided financial investment and expertise in the form of seconded staff, worked closely in designing garments and helping develop the technology to make them efficiently. As a result of decades of mutual aid 'a relationship of trust was established. . . . It was often said that M&S was Britain's biggest manufacturer without owning any factories and that their suppliers were retailers with no shops'.[27] Roughly 50 per cent of all Baird's production was for M&S and they grew, contracted, refitted, held back and expanded output pretty much for the benefit, and at the behest and bellow of M&S. It was close to a marriage but one without any prenuptial contract signed. The skein of communications, interactions, dialogues and disquisitions over the years make for a complex romance that ended abruptly when, due to a changed commercial environment, M&S abruptly terminated the relationship without notice, simply by not ordering any clothes when the season came due.

The Court of Appeal had decided against Baird's claim of implied contract and denied that estoppel – detrimental reliance – was available in English law. The feel of the judgment can be gleaned swiftly from Lord Mance:

> Objectively, the only sensible analysis of the present situation is in my judgment that the parties had an extremely good long-term commercial

---

[26] Linda Mulcahy and Cathy Andrews, '*Baird Textile Holdings v Marks & Spencer Plc* [2003] (Baroness Mulandrew)' in Rosemary Hunter et al. (eds), *Feminist Judgments: From Theory to Practice* (London: Hart, 2010) at 189. The Court of Appeal decision is *Baird Textile Holdings v Marks & Spencer Plc* [2001] EWCA Civ 274, [2002] 1 All ER (Comm) 737.

[27] Mulandrew, 'Baird', at 189.

relationship, but not one which they ever sought to express, or which the court would ever seek to express, in terms of long-term contractual obligations.[28]

Lord Judge, for it is he, Judge Judge judging again, adds that as far as estoppel as a cause of action is concerned, with questionable felicity of expression:

> However settled the law may appear to be, one of its strengths is that the possibility of development, or change, remains. In my view, even for the purposes of [summary judgment], we must apply the law as it is, not as it *may* possibly one day become (my emphasis).[29]

Needless to say, M&S were also deemed, objectively, to have no requisite intention to create legal relations. The two main points on appeal are thus the court's sense of objectivity and the anterograde character of the judicial sense of the future, their default of imagination.

The object and objective of the arrangement is sartorial. These are tailors, designers of clothes, cutters of cloth who measure and trim: the length of the leg, and the girth of the blouse, the frock and frippery of Schreber's *armentarium* of frou frou accessories. When Lord Mance adopts the 'sensible' position it is one that is distinctly lacking in sensorium and sensibility. There is indeed little of sense at all in the judgments and no recognition, objective or other, of clothes sense, and, as Carlyle puts it in *Sartor Resartus*, that most necessary work for any judgment of dress, the court evidently has 'the Tarantula dance ... has no ear left for Literature'.[30] The court is addressing a question of dress, customs and costumes, clothes and character and is claiming to do what is sensible, the fitting thing, but the judgments lack any sense of the appropriate style or, to borrow from Carlyle again 'all Forms whereby Spirit manifests itself to sense, whether outwardly or in the imagination, are Clothes ... the Pomp and Authority of Law ... more properly a Vesture and Raiment'.[31] The objective, in sum, is also subjective, just as the absence of feeling – numbness – is a sense and

---

28 *Baird v Marks & Spencer*, para. 69 (Lord Mance).
29 Ibid., para. 55 (Lord Judge).
30 Thomas Carlyle, Sartor Resartus: *The Life and Opinions of Herr Teufelsdröckh* (1833–4) (Boston: James Munroe and Co, 1836) Book I at ch 5. There is, of course, François Broé, *Analogia iuris ad vestem* (1636), and then more recently Gary Watt, *Dress, Law and the Naked Truth: A Cultural Study of Fashion and Form* (London: Bloomsbury, 2012).
31 *Sartor Resartus*, Bk III at ch 9.

a feeling. The expectations of the parties, the desire and the history of co-operation, the flexibility and refiguration of production and sale over time, the mutual aid and imbrication of the parties all indicate, if anything, something more than contract, duration and something that common law in particular should have appreciated, namely an unwritten law – *ius non scriptum* – in the mode of dress and deportment, custom and costume, parties pleated together.

The feminist Judge Mulandrew picks up the point upon appeal. There is an article of dress and shelter that is of paramount importance in inclement conditions, namely the umbrella. As Carlyle observes, it is unnecessary during dry weather but must be carried and unfurled in wet.[32] As the going had become difficult, as the augurs and weather changed, the apotropaic device and article of proper attire, the umbrella became an understandably and bespoke form now necessary. It is unfurled in the Feminist Judgment as a sartorial requisite:

> The umbrella contract is a device through which the interests of one party become the interests of both. It reflects the need for co-operation in the joint production or acquisition of wealth in which long-term contracts are seen as being geared towards mutual futures. The umbrella contract is capable of reflecting the essence of the agreement and the ties that bind commercial parties much more effectively than a string of spot contracts.[33]

A long-term relationship between clothiers, the intimacy of apparel, the trust, interdependence, co-operation and shared goals of the espoused businesses would, in sum, be unthinkable without that essential accoutrement and accessory of good style, the brolly. The parties had operated 'under the shadow of the umbrella' and a contract could be implied from its folds. In more formal language: 'The umbrella contract articulates what have been called a high order of shared conventions which comprise customary, expected, legal and non-legal rules and principles.'[34] Here we hit the key point, the ferrule of the cane, which is that these are shadows, phantasms of judgment, because according to Judge Judge these umbrellas are not the law *as it*

---

32 Ibid., ch 3: 'To us, at that period, Herr Heuschrecke seemed one of those purse-mouthed, crane-necked, clean-brushed, pacific individuals, perhaps insufficiently distinguished in society by this fact, that, in dry weather or in wet, "they never appear without their umbrella".' Hofrath Heuschrecke was Boswell to Professor Teufelsdröckh's Dr Johnson. Gary Watt, *Naked Truth*, makes the point that the umbrella is clothes and shelter enfolded in one.
33 *Feminist Judgments*, at 201 (Baroness Mulandrew).
34 Ibid., at 200 (Baroness Mulandrew).

is but, uttered in a tone of disbelief, 'the law as it *may possibly* one day become'.

The Wild Law Judgments project suggests a transitional method of taking chances and grasping opportunities. Cullinan describes this as attending to 'the flashes of wild law in existing legal doctrines, the re-examining of all legal rules and conventions with wide open, wild eyes'.[35] How very appropriate, sartorially, to resort to the pleats of an umbrella, to what the French term the *parapluie*, the shield and canopy against the rain. It is however more than simply a jurisliterary elegance that is in play in this shift. The *Spirit of Clothes* is self-consciously composed in parallel to the *Spirit of Laws*, and it is in its inner recesses, in the practices and choices of cut and cloth that its philosophy is to be found:

> If the Cut betoken Intellect and Talent, so does the Color betoken Temper and Heart. In all which, among nations as among individuals, there is an incessant, though infinitely complex working of Cause and Effect: every snip of the Scissors has been regulated and prescribed by ever-active Influences, which doubtless to Intelligences of a superior order are neither invisible nor illegible.

Carlyle goes on to make the point that such 'Cause-and-Effect Philosophy of Clothes, as of Laws, were probably a comfortable winter-evening entertainment: nevertheless, for inferior Intelligences, like men, such Philosophies have always seemed uninstructive enough'.[36] Cause and effect, chop logic, the objectivism of cause and effect is much less sensible than an appreciation of colour and cut, temper and talent, if what is in issue is the law of clothes. For this reason, a materialist judgment, here a feminist judgment, grabs the brolly, picks up that mad instrument, the *parapluie*, so as not to forget it, so as to have some protection. The umbrella is the matterphorical means for apprehending the sartorial relation and for taking up the spirit of clothes in a seam and lapel that recognizes the post human context and collar of this long-sleeved dispute.

The umbrella is an imaginative choice of device. In pataphysical terms it can be the vehicle of flight and of floating, a sword and a shield, an opening and unfurling. Judge Judge's view, that we apply the law as it

---

35 Cormac Cullinan, *Wild Law* (Siber Ink, 2002) at 10.
36 *Sartor Resartus*, ch. 5.

is and not as it may be, is one that seemingly lacks a sensibility of the future, of the potential of interpretation and the mobility of the art of justice as one of jurisliterary interpretation. For Forcadel, poetics was the Archimedean point where literary imagination raised law to the zenith of its capacity and folded mundane rules into the higher aesthetic principles of creative potential, into the company of the fine arts, the apogees of human and posthuman expression. Decided by an umbrella is a perfect pataphysical expression of method and allows us to recollect that the principal statement of pataphysics comes in the form of a response to a legal process, *Exploits and Opinions of Dr Faustroll, Pataphysician* beginning of course with a summons for non-payment of rent and then the impounding of 27 books and diverse prints and posters.[37] The books and the art impounded are the avenue to pataphysical invention insofar as the absurd precision of legalese proves entirely inadequate to its task of restraint, and palls when compared to the mad lucidity of artistic expression permeated with possibility and fecundity of imaginings. The dense prose of legal forms is undone by the anarchic vision of a language free of denotation. The literal becomes littoral, labile and liminal and, as we know, Faustroll then takes to the sea upon a boat which is a sieve.

Jarry's definition of 'pataphysics as the science of imaginary solutions can also act as an optimistic and progressive definition of the potential of jurisliterature. Recollect that pataphysics is predicated upon an examination 'of the laws governing exceptions, and will explain the universe supplementary to this one; or, less ambitiously, will describe a universe which can be – and perhaps should be – envisaged in place of the traditional one. . .'.[38] As the point of intersection of aesthetics and jurisprudence, poetics and law, the jurisliterary expands our concept of the juridical, grabbing umbrellas, weaving texts, vivifying divinities, seeing ghosts, posting pictures in judgments, and in Schreber's case attending to the world of the infinitely little in which homunculi climb up hir legs and lift their eyelids. The intellective strategy is one of defamiliarization, one that attends to the mobility of thought and expands the perspectives from which possibility is viewed, from infinitely small to exponentially enlarged, from that of the viewer to that of the viewed. The traditional perception of legal method, as espoused

---

37 Alfred Jarry, *Exploits and Opinions of Dr Faustroll, Pataphysician* (Boston: Exact Change, 1996). Andrew Hugill, *Pataphysics: A Useless Guide* (Boston: MIT Press, 2012) provides biographical background and philosophical context.

38 Jarry, *Faustroll*, at 21–2.

emphatically by Judge Judge, that law must be applied as it is, not as it may possibly be, is displaced by a ludic space of the *as if*, which is that of oneiric visions, reveries, inversions and exceptions. The nomic view of the world is but one, highly constrained, backward looking, perspective upon what is conceived as an essentially static and closed juridical realm. The role of imagination is that of introducing alternate and more mobile domains of transitional being into the strictures of legality. As Feyerabend famously formulated the principle: 'we need a dream-world in order to discover the features of the real world we think we inhabit (and which may actually be just another dream-world)'.[39]

The future is the madness of the present. Novelty takes the form of contemporary exceptions, imaginary hypotheses that establish the possible as credible. Much of what Jarry imagined, from telepathic letters, floating sieves, the world of the infinitely little, euphorisms, pataphysical laughter, the definition of the divinity as 'the tangential point between zero and infinity', dialogues with a protagonist who can only say 'ha, ha', the law of the ascension of a vacuum toward a periphery, have all proved peculiarly prescient in a manner quite alien to what *is*, the norm at the time of their being written. There are always circumstances when the rule should be ignored, suspended, expanded or contracted, its opposite adopted as imaginative excursions, thought experiments that transform paradigms of normality. That was Jarry's genius. It was also Schreber's brilliance because no jurist in the 1890s really dared to imagine that a senior male judge could become a woman, that picturing was an alternate form of reasoning, that the aura of jurists and gaolers could be their condemnation, that visions have heuristic value, that machines are oppressive *dispositifs*, that soul voluptuousness matters, that madness could co-exist with law, or that all things are connected by nerves and rays extending and entwining bodies and nature throughout the universe. Rats, foxes, birds. Earth, humans, sky.

---

39 Paul Feyerabend, *Against Method: Outline of an Anarchist Theory of Knowledge* (London: Verso, 1975/2002) at 22.

Epilogue

From her to eternity. Grab an umbrella, turn out the lights in the haunted house, take a photograph, paint a picture, sprinkle petals in front of the altar to Shiva and borrow from Shakespeare, why not: 'The weight of this sad time we must obey / Speak what we feel, not what we ought to say'. The long-term project of jurisliterature has been that of rendering law aesthetically pleasing and ethically appropriate. To bring imagination to the normative practices and decisional dictates of legal actors is not simply to beautify the edifice of legality, it is also to engage creatively in the performance of justice. Mellifluous motions, jovial judgments, palatable pleas, decorous decisions raise the tone and contribute to the decorum of ceremony that distinguishes law from mere administration. Legal elegance, *elegantia iuris* as it used to be termed, the poetics of *latinitas* meaning historical and philological knowledge of the tradition, combine to proffer the art in law and to fashion the equity with which to shape legal decisions. Imagination opens the doors of the institution to creativity and novelty as well as to that felicity of expression and aptitude of figuration that allows the particular circumstances of a given case to be rendered – painted – justly.

Marett Leiboff, thespian and lawyer, in developing her account of theatrical jurisprudence, insists upon the importance of training the body, augmenting the senses, to notice, to be aware of the immediate environment, persons, events, even before becoming conscious of their happening. Attending to pre-conscious cognition, involuntary smiles, blushes, laughter, desire and fear as heuristic facets of *in vivo* juridical interactions provides essential information as well as embedding the performance of law in the viscera and particularity of the given occasion. Theatrical training inculcates both the capacity and the skill to access the intimate recesses of the body, to listen to the senses, to be aware of the skin and other receptors before knowing why they are reacting. Leiboff describes a seminar in which she mentions an Australian politician who had been at the centre of a widely publicized scandal in Queensland. One of the audience members, Maks, an

Australian, leans forward and smiles as he listens but when questioned later was utterly unaware of his smile. Noticing the grin, observing the smirk, and being aware that one is responding in that manner embeds the exchange in the bodies and biographies of the participants and brings a haptic and sensory apprehension, a more plural and mobile attentiveness to the circumstances. Maks, the participant who smiled had remembered the story and the events which Leiboff had been discussing although, as she points out, he was too young to have been present in Queensland at that time. The smile, nonetheless, conveys the affectivity of encounter, and signals interest, proximity and a certain connection that will impact respondent and response in the drama of the seminar, in the account of the case, in actions taken and judgments made in relation to those confluences, confrontations and events.

Embedding the participants in the encounter, with its variable theatrical, social, scholarly, juridical implications, means being present, responding bodily, noticing the corporeal intimations that precede conscious iteration and, at the risk of repetition: 'it is not that the body remembers, but that *the body itself is memory*'.[1] The prosopographic smile, the leaning forwards and the grimace on the visage, the change of aspect, are symptoms, corporeal signs that the participant has been located and has engaged physically and mentally with the subject matter of the encounter, connected to the event, and is actively present in the exchange. What happens when law is enacted, when legal actions occur, is not abstract but rather imbricates persons at a particular time and in a particular place, with its atmosphere, sounds, colours, costumes, images, and architecture. That these are generally unconsciously absorbed simply reflects a juristic tendency to disembodiment and lack of awareness which Leiboff persuasively impugns in her revival of post-dramatic, poor theatre as an essential methodological and didactic tool in training lawyers to attend, to listen and notice more than themselves, beyond themselves, in themselves.

Theatrical jurisprudence, the present tense and tensor of the performative falls for Leiboff within the parameters of jurisography, an antipodean approach to legal theory which insists upon the incorpora-

---

1 Marett Leiboff, *Theatrical Jurisprudence*, 109 et seq. The term jurisography come from A. Genovese and S. McVeigh, 'Nineteen eighty three: a jurisographic report on *Commonwealth v Tasmania.*' (2015) 24(1) *Griffith Law Review* 68, defined at 70: 'The duties that attach to the office of jurisographer involve examining how jurisprudence was written, thought and practiced in time and place and paying attention to how those traditions have been inherited.'

tion of the land, the time, place, song lines and locality of law so as to reconstruct what she appropriately terms 'law's lost presence'. As Hans-Thies Lehmann formulates it: 'no law (and certainly no law that is "good" or "democratic") stands on a blank slate; it always includes earlier and coming generations . . . [and] enlists the extralegal power to which it owes its origin and continued existence'.[2] Temporality and geography, lives lived lawfully, in recognition of juristic history and geography impel an acknowledgement and theoretical appreciation of the material conditions and cultural work that lawyers perform. Accepting responsibility for the lost dimensions visceral immediacy and the narrative of encounter makes the jurisographic account of legal events an endeavour that rubs against the grain of law's closure and the positivistic abstraction of case reports and other interpretative acts. Restoration of the climate and critical context, the painstaking and generally oppositional expression of the details of persons, things and actions embedded in the flesh of history constitutes a minor jurisprudence, an excluded language that fights for its own disciplinary place, the rights of the deterritorialized language, the minority group, foreign law, different gestures, other visions.

Jurisography forms a significant emergent part of the jurisliterary and of its endeavour to imaginatively convey the visceral reality of law to new generations in novel modes and media. The jurisliterary embraces the interdisciplinary and in its contemporary focus upon *trans* discourses seeks constantly to facilitate and relay the experiences that underlie minor jurisprudences, the excluded languages, hidden figures, denied materiality and cultural forms that inscribe the returning peripheries of law's imperial gaze. Jurisliterature expands the jurisographic by embracing not only the ontographic and posthuman perspectives of the transitional but also the rotating community of disciplines and diversity of media and relays impacting and altering the matter and frame of contemporary legality. The jurisliterary incorporates all those practices and methods that can aid in the materialization of law through attention to affect and body, theatre and dance, certainly, but also through techniques of viewing and distributing the sensible that are made available through film, videography, streaming, online, as text and image, sound and colour, motion and emotion. The graphosphere, the predominance of the textual, is exponentially expanded by the new *dispositifs* of the visual and the virtual. To be

---

2 Hans-Thies Lehmann, *Tragedy and Dramatic Theatre* [trans. Erik Butler] (London: Routledge, 2016) at 107.

meaningful as a humanist venture, the jurisliterary must expand into novelty of media and methods and imaginatively combine new forms and relays as aspects of legal practice, the acts and entities of law. It is not just law's past that is hidden, requiring painstaking reconstruction, but rather that such a task is necessary because the everyday of contemporary juridism, in multiple little acts of denial and negation, obscures the living characters and wounds, the struggles and, yes, the pain and death (Cover should not be covered) over which it presides and administrates.

The jurisliterary provides its now multi-modal and pluri-cultural account of the antique tradition as it mutates, bends and transitions in the novel contexts of new generations and accelerating social change. We see law, we hear, smell and feel law, we walk the line as images of bodies, as the materiality of spectres, as humans in a posthuman viral and virtual reality.[3] Accelerating change suggests a technique of bricolage in which the jurist takes advice and concepts from film, videography, media theory, fine art, pulp fiction and television, *lex populi* at the level of law's increasingly dispersed trajectories of materialization. That is why, in the last chapter, the analysis of a commercial dispute over the quality of cloth picked up and took off from the perspective of the textile, and why looking at a long-term, and intimately intricate commercial supply relationship, the interpretation reached for an umbrella. It was not nature that had to be kept out. It was the inclemency of the stronger party who had for three decades controlled the development and practices of the manufacturer of the clothing that they sold. Zarathustra, being fond of the elements, may not have required an umbrella, but those engaged in long-term relations, commercial spouses, *de futuro* in the old language, may well expect, if not Mary Poppins, at least a version of the umbrella that she utilizes so adeptly.[4] The technique is one of materializing the matter in dispute, of acting prudently, which is to say through experience and conduct that engages with the actors and materiality of the dispute, the fall of the case, or the frame and features of governance.

---

3 On the ambulatory and velociped dimensions of the lawscape, there is no better essay than the funambulous Andreas Philippopoulos-Mihalopoulos, 'To have to do with law: an essay', in Philippopoulos-Mihalopoulos (ed.), *Routledge Handbook on Law and Theory* (London: Routledge, 2019)

4 See Jacques Derrida, *Spurs: Nietzsche's Styles / Éperons: Les Styles de Nietzsche* (Chicago: Chicago University Press, 1981) for an extended analysis of the fragment found amongst Neitzsche's remains, a note stating simply 'I have forgotten my umbrella.'

Law creates a world, structured juristically as persons, bonds and actions. These are imaginal categories, spectral and material, they constitute the life of images amongst images, faces on the screen, nanobots to black holes, brittlestar to sound barrier. Where one is, lodged in the subatomic of neutrons and protons or falling to earth from space, skydiving 25 miles at a top speed of some 843 mph, will likely dictate the laws that govern and the imaginal laws generated. Something new matters. The task of jurisliterature, as framed in this advancing introduction, is that of engaging with and endeavouring to shape the juristic formulation of such encounters and events. The imagination of lawyers needs constant scrutiny, criticism and renewal. This can use the tools of literary criticism, linguistic analysis, textual theory, cinema studies, archiveology, videography, alternative repute resolution, and similar, but I have preferred to attend to the jurist in the literary, to what the humanist lawyers have sent on.

The scope of the jurisliterary could be greatly expanded. It could include the numerous and valuable works of lawyers who become novelists, poets, social theorists, snoutfigs and gardeners. Exit orientated jurists, ex lawyers have a huge amount to offer, and frequently provide significant inspiration but belong to a different though interrelated genre and are frequently cited, worked with, borrowed and incorporated into the company of disciplines that jurists access and exercise in their diverse works, be it opera, fiction, film, photography, painting, sculpture, ballet, graffiti or spontaneous performance. In that one cannot include all arts and disciplines in the *bonae artes* of jurisliterary interventions the pressing question becomes that of choice and change. The critic of law is frequently engaged in seeking to escape law, to fill the hole at the heart of the legal with the wealth of another discipline. Such still, however, requires proximity to the juridical, a sense of a future, institutional belonging, an investment in the interior recesses of the arts of law. And so, envoi, 'pity me not but lend thy serious hearing to what I shall unfold'.

Index

Adam 34, 35
aequitas 54
aesthetic ix–xi, xiv–xvi, 5, 6, 13–17, 45, 47, 68–9, 71, 83, 89, 94, 107, 109
Agamben, Giorgio 44, 62–3
Alice 63, 65
Allegheny College v National Chautauqua Bank 51
allegory xv, 4, 44–8, 51–5, 63–6, 101
allotropes 98
anarchy 23, 97
Aneau, Barthélemy 19
angels 30, 31, 35
antiquae fabulae xi–xii, 42
apparel 92–5
arcana imperii 32
architecture 16, 24–7, 32–4, 39
Aristodemou, Maria viii, 109
Aristotle 8, 45
as if 1, 108
Atkins, Lord 39, 40, 63–4
audite et alterem partem 33–5
auctoritates poetarum xiv, 6, 35, 54
Austen, Jane 48, 51, 60
Aylmer, Bishop 14

Baigent v Random House 1–3
Baird Textiles v Marks and Spencers 102–104
Bakhtin, Mikhail 9–10
Behrmann, Carolin 43
Bible 33–6, 39, 60
Blackstone, Sir William 2
Binder, Guyora viii, 69
Bingham, Lord 37, 39
Bowdler 58–60
Boyd White, James viii, 69

Broé, François 104
Browning v Johnson 51
Byrne, Susan x–xi

cameras in court 72–6
Cardozo, Benjamin N. 50–51
Carlyle, Thomas 104–106
Carroll, Lewis 63, 65–6
Chambers v Director of Public Prosecutions 55–61
charlatans (legal) 19
Christ 24, 27, 40, 52, 69
Church of the Holy Trinity v U. S. 35–6
Cicero 63, 67, 101
Clare and Others v Bedelis 77–9
Coccia, Emanuele 99–100
Coke, Sir Edward 14, 15, 20, 27–8, 39, 40
comedy *see* humour
commandments 43
Communications Act 2003 55, 58
corporography x, 90–95, 98, 110
consideration 49–52
contempt of court 33–4, 73–6
contract 48–53, 100–102
Cormack, Bradin xi, 21
corpus iuris civilis 13, 26–7, 29, 70, 92–5
covering 48–50
Cowell, John 20
Criminal Justice Act 1925 73
critical legal studies 11–13, 23, 24
criticism
    legal 1, 20, 23–4, 73, 77
    literary ix, 2, 11, 42, 69, 113
Cullinan, Cormac 106
cryptogram *see* enigma

Da Vinci Code 1–2, 4–5
Darling, Charles xii
Daumal, René xiii, 38
Davies, Sir John 20, 30
Debray, Régis 68
Defence Powers Regulations 1939 63–4
Deleuze, Giles 45–6, 66
Derrida, Jacques 49, 54–5, 112
dialogue viii–ix, 4–5, 7–13, 16, 54
Didi-Huberman, George 68–70
Digest (of Justinian) xii, 31, 53, 56, 70
Director of Public Prosecution v Chambers 54–6, 59–62
disciplines 10–11, 13, 17, 60–61, 97
  circulus disciplinarum 61, 98
dissimulation 44–5, 60
dispositif 25–6, 43–4, 58, 79, 108, 111
dogma 31, 81
Dodderidge, Sir John 20, 31, 43
Donoghue v Stevenson 102
Dugdale, William 29
druids xiv, 14, 15, 29

education 6, 13, 18, 21
effect (*effectus*) 44, 62–3, 65
elegantia iuris xiv, 17–18, 21, 22–3, 47, 96, 98, 109
emblems 14, 27, 69–71
enargeia 67
enigma 3–4
ens imaginarium 94
equity 54
Evans, David 32
Eve 34, 35
exceptions 107–108

Facebook 56, 75
Faustroll 106–108
Feminist Judgments 103–105
Feyerabend, Paul 108
Fisher, Mark 38
Freud, Sigmund xvi, 46, 49, 70, 83–4
Fry, Stephen 56
fiction 2–3, 62
  legal 3, 42, 62
Finch, Henry 30
Forcadel, Etienne 98, 107

Fortescue, Sir John 9, 29
friendship 8, 11–13, 101
Fulbeck, William 14, 40

Gabel, Peter 11–13
Gaia 96
Gandorfer, Daniela 13, 27–8, 97
gargantua 13
gender dysphoria 90–99
Gennaro, Giuseppe xiv, 15–16, 18
Germain, Christopher St. 11
Ghaidan v Godin-Mendoza 64
ghosts 22–4, 31–2, 38
Ginsberg, Carlo 49
gods 36–40, 69

habitus 30, 68, 97
Haigh v Brooks 51
Haldar, Piyel 34
Hayaert, Valérie 71
Heher, Judge 47–53
hierarchy 24–6, 31–2
hierophants 23
HM Attorney General v Kasim Davey 56
Hobbes, Thomas 30
Hochster v De la Tour 52
Homer 60
Housman, A.E. 63–4
humanism 18–20, 43–8, 61, 69–70, 113
humour xii–xiv, 5, 11, 21, 57–62
Humpty Dumpty 63, 65
humus/earth 28, 39

image viii, xv, 24–5, 67–72, 76–82, 84–8, 99–100
  and text 77–8, 83–4
  imago decidendi 83
  ius imaginum 6, 71, 81
  vivified 37–8, 43, 67, 88
imaginal xi, 4, 12, 60, 68–9, 77, 83, 87–9, 93–4, 99, 113
imperson 94
Inns of Court 31, 103
institution 5–13, 15, 16, 20, 42–3, 70–71, 76, 96
  instituere vitam 16, 43–4, 47
Institutes of Justinian xi–xii, 8, 70

instruction 15, 47
Isidore of Seville 43
Investor's Compensation Scheme v W. Bromwich Building Soc. 65–6
iura imaginaria 6

Janus 14
Jarry, Alfred xiii, 107–109
jokes 56–61, 101
Judge Judge 56, 57, 104, 106, 108
jurisconsults xii, 15
jurisdiction x–xi, 15, 34, 46, 48–50
jurisliterature ix–xi, xii, 5, 12–14, 20, 45–8, 51–6, 58–63, 67, 69–70, 75–8, 88–9, 95–100, 107–109
    defined ix–xi
jurisography vii, x–xi, 110–111
jurisprudence
    island of 15–16, 18–19
    minor 45–8, 111
    poetic viii, x, xii, 3, 5, 6–8, 18, 21–4, 62–4, 83, 97–8, 107
    theatrical x, xv, 4, 43–4, 57–63, 84–7, 102, 110–111
    and transition xv–xvi, 90–99
Jurists
    ancient xii, xiv, 6, 9, 11, 21
    modern 11–13, 15, 40, 62–4, 70–72
    republic of 5, 13, 15, 17–19, 20, 64
    transitional xvi, 90–99,
justice 18–19, 21, 45–6, 53–4, 98–100, 107
    Retinal 83
Justinian xi, 26–7, 53, 56, 70
justissima tellus xiv, xv, 28, 36–8, 96

Kafka, Franz 25
Kennedy, Duncan 11–13
King Lear 59–61
Khorakiwala, Rahela 26

Latin xiv, 24–5, 27, 31–34, 50, 54, 101, 109
laughter xii–xiv, xvi, 11, 16, 47, 108–109
law
    affect xii, xv
    anterograde 104
    clothes xiv, 16, 73, 86, 99–100, 103–106
    common 29
    desire ix, xii, xiv, 82, 90–94
    faith 36–7, 39
    history xii, xiv, 32, 69–75
    humanism x–x, 17, 61
    literature viii, 52–4, 60–63, 85
    psychiatric 90–92
    Roman 24, 29, 31, 39
    sartorial 104–106
    sex 53, 80, 92–3, 95
    tablets xiv, 13, 24, 43
    traditions x–xii
    trans xv, 90–95, 98, 99–103, 108, 111
    unwritten 15, 26–8, 30, 32, 34, 39–40, 105
    vacuum 107–108
    wild x, xiii–xiv, 13, 36, 102, 106
    youth xi–xii, 8

lawyers *see* jurists
Legendre, Pierre 16, 81
Leiboff, Marett x, 102–103, 109–111
Lehmann, Hans-Thies 111
Levine v Blumenthal 47–50, 52–3
literalism 6, 17–18, 24, 45, 65, 74
lex terrae xiv, xiv, 15, 27–30, 35–40, 96
litterarisation (of law) 5, 17, 46–50
Liversidge v Sir John Anderson 63
Lyotard, Jean-François 84
Lyttleton, Sir Thomas 15

MacNeil, Bill viii
madness 90–95
malapropism xv, 65–6
Manderson, Desmond 60, 68
Mannai Investment v Eagle Star Life Assurance Co Ltd 66
marginal 49–50
maxims 31, 81
materialism xv, 3–4, 27–9, 80, 97–9
matterphor xii, xv, 13, 16, 27–8, 36–9, 44–6, 55, 63, 81, 98, 106–107
medicine 6, 90–95
Memoirs of My Nervous Illness 90–92, 94–8

metaphor xii, xv, 44–6, 101
Minkkinen, Panu 45–6
minor 46–9, 111
Minucius 18–19
morbus juridicus 91–3
mos americanus iuris docendi xi
mos britannicus iuris docendi xi, 10, 14, 15, 32, 34
mos gallicus iuris docendi xi, 14
mos hispanicus iuris docendi x–xi
mos italicus iuris docendi 14
mos literatus iuris docendi x
Mulcahy, Linda 26, 102–104
music xiv, 5–8, 11–12, 23, 94, 97
MWB Business Exchange Centres v Rock Advertising 51

Narcissus 82, 88
Nietzsche, Friedrich 112
Nomos x–xi, 28, 30, 35, 39, 108

oikonomia 44, 91
Old Bailey 25–6
ontography 92, 96
Ovid 82, 83

pataphysics xiii, xvi, 38, 103, 106–108
Pennsy Supply Inc. v American Ash Recycling Corp. 51
Periphrasis 50–51
Perkins, William 31–2
Peters, Julie Stone viii–ix
Philippopoulos-Mihalopoulos, Andreas 25, 112
photographs 72–83, 86–8
Picton, HHJ 75
picturing 93–4
Plato xiv, 6–9, 11, 18, 21
Plowden, Edmund 42
poethics viii, xii, 55
poiesis 5, 24–5, 42
political theology 94
Pope Gregory 30
Posner, Richard 84–8
precedent x–xi, 24, 46
Preciado, Paul 96
prolegomena (to law) 21

Psalms 25
Pugsley, David xii
Puttenham, George 44
Pythagoras 5

Quintilian 67

R v Frederick Henry Seddon 73–4
R v Somerset County Council ex parte Frewings 36
R v University of Cambridge 33
Ram, Lord 37–8
regimen animarum 43–4
Republic of Letters 5, 14–19, 20
rhetoric 1, 16, 42, 44–5, 48–51, 52–5, 65–6, 68, 88
Rhetorica ad Herennium 67
Rowden, Emma 26
Rogers, Nicole 102–103
Rogers of Earlsferry, Lord 64–5
Ruggles, George 34–5

Saint Germain 54
Sanders, Mark 90–91
Sartor Resartus 104–106
Schreber, Daniel Paul xvi, 90–99, 107, 108
  Miss Schreber 90, 93, 94, 99
sciography 16, 57, 83, 105
Selden, John 14
Senneton 70
serio-ludere xii
serpent 35
Shakespeare, William 22, 24, 54–5, 59–61, 109
Shelley, Percy Bysshe 21–3
Shiva 109
Siddiq v Suresh 37–8
Sidney, Sir Philip 5
Sikhs for Justice v Badal 85–9
Simonides 67
Siva 37–8
Smith, Peter 1–4, 18, 23
Solicitor General v Cox and Parker Stokes 75
sovereignty 13
spectacle 89

spectres 22–3, 24
Spinoza, Baruch 96
spousals *de futuro* 51–2
Sri Sabhanayagar Temple, Chidambaram v State of Tamil Nadu 37–8
Stambovsky v Ackley 22–3
Starkey, Thomas 9
Stewart, Ghilchrist James 45
Swinburne, Henry 64, 65

Teissier-Ensminger, Anne ix, 5–9, 17, 46–8
text x–xi, 11, 13, 15, 21, 26–7, 30, 100–103
Textile v A..BMH 99–102
Through the Looking Glass 62–3
time immemorial *see* time out of mind
time out of mind xiv, 14–15, 30, 34, 52
transgression 56–8
transhumusian 98
Twelve Tables 13, 24
Twitter 55–62

Ubi amor, ibi oculos 84
Ulpian 21
umbrellas 105–106, 108, 109, 112

V for Vendetta 25
Vaihinger, Hans 94

vera philosophia 19–20
verba visibilia 70
veritas falsa 44
vestigium, imago, similitudo 81
Vico, Giambattista 6, 18, 24, 45
videosphere 68
viserbality 77
vision 25–6, 82, 87–9
vividæ rationes 88
visiones 67
Vismann, Cornelia 72–3
Vives, Jan-Luis 5
void 30
Vokes v Murray Inc 54

Watt, Gary 16, 99–100, 103, 104, 105
Weisberg, Richard viii, xii
Weisberg, Robert viii, 69
White, James-Boyd 8, 69
Whitehouse, Edward 31
Wild Law 102, 106
Williams v Roffey 51
wool 101–104
Word, the 69

Yoshino, Kenji 8, 48
youth (eager for law) xi, 8

Zarathustra 112
Zodiak 5

Titles in the **Elgar Advanced Introductions** series include:

International Political Economy
Benjamin J. Cohen

The Austrian School of Economics
Randall G. Holcombe

Cultural Economics
Ruth Towse

Law and Development
Michael J. Trebilcock and Mariana Mota Prado

International Humanitarian Law
Robert Kolb

International Trade Law
Michael J. Trebilcock

Post Keynesian Economics
J.E. King

International Intellectual Property
Susy Frankel and Daniel J. Gervais

Public Management and Administration
Christopher Pollitt

Organised Crime
Leslie Holmes

Nationalism
Liah Greenfeld

Social Policy
Daniel Béland and Rianne Mahon

Globalisation
Jonathan Michie

Entrepreneurial Finance
Hans Landström

International Conflict and Security Law
Nigel D. White

Comparative Constitutional Law
Mark Tushnet

International Human Rights Law
Dinah L. Shelton

Entrepreneurship
Robert D. Hisrich

International Tax Law
Reuven S. Avi-Yonah

Public Policy
B. Guy Peters

The Law of International Organizations
Jan Klabbers

International Environmental Law
Ellen Hey

International Sales Law
Clayton P. Gillette

Corporate Venturing
Robert D. Hisrich

Public Choice
Randall G. Holcombe

Private Law
Jan M. Smits

Consumer Behavior Analysis
Gordon Foxall

Behavioral Economics
John F. Tomer

Cost-Benefit Analysis
Robert J. Brent

Environmental Impact Assessment
Angus Morrison-Saunders

Comparative Constitutional Law
Second Edition
Mark Tushnet

National Innovation Systems
Cristina Chaminade, Bengt-Åke Lundvall and Shagufta Haneef

Ecological Economics
Matthias Ruth

Private International Law and Procedure
Peter Hay

Freedom of Expression
Mark Tushnet

Law and Globalisation
Jaakko Husa

Regional Innovation Systems
Bjørn T. Asheim, Arne Isaksen and Michaela Trippl

International Political Economy
Second Edition
Benjamin J. Cohen

International Tax Law
Second Edition
Reuven S. Avi-Yonah

Social Innovation
Frank Moulaert and Diana MacCallum

The Creative City
Charles Landry

International Trade Law
Michael J. Trebilcock and Joel Trachtman

European Union Law
Jacques Ziller

Planning Theory
Robert A. Beauregard

Tourism Destination Management
Chris Ryan

International Investment Law
August Reinisch

Sustainable Tourism
David Weaver

Austrian School of Economics
Second Edition
Randall G. Holcombe

U.S. Criminal Procedure
Christopher Slobogin

Platform Economics
Robin Mansell and W. Edward Steinmueller

Public Finance
Vito Tanzi

Feminist Economics
Joyce P. Jacobsen

Human Dignity and Law
James R. May and Erin Daly

Space Law
Frans G. von der Dunk

National Accounting
John M. Hartwick

Legal Research Methods
Ernst Hirsch Ballin

Privacy Law
Megan Richardson

International Human Rights Law
Second Edition
Dinah L. Shelton

Law and Artificial Intelligence
Woodrow Barfield and Ugo Pagallo

Politics of International Human Rights
David P. Forsythe

Community-based Conservation
Fikret Berkes

Global Production Networks
Neil M. Coe

Mental Health Law
Michael L. Perlin

Law and Literature
Peter Goodrich

ELGAR ADVANCED INTRODUCTIONS: LAW

www.advancedintros.com

Access the whole eBook collection at a cost effective price for law students at your institution.

Email: **sales@e-elgar.co.uk** for more information